LIBRA
24 SEPTEMBER – 23 OCTOBER

All Rights Reserved including the right of reproduction in whole or in part in any form. This edition is published by arrangement with Harlequin Enterprises II B.V./S.à.r.l. The text of this publication or any part thereof may not be reproduced or transmitted in any form or by any means, electronic or mechanical, including photocopying, recording, storage in an information retrieval system, or otherwise, without the written permission of the publisher.

This book is sold subject to the condition that it shall not, by way of trade or otherwise, be lent, resold, hired out or otherwise circulated without the prior consent of the publisher in any form of binding or cover other than that in which it is published, and without a similar condition including this condition being imposed on the subsequent purchaser.

® and ™ are trademarks owned and used by the trademark owner and/or its licensee. Trademarks marked with ® are registered with the United Kingdom Patent Office and/or the Office for Harmonisation in the Internal Market and in other countries.

First published in Great Britain 2013
by Mills & Boon, an imprint of Harlequin (UK) Limited,
Eton House, 18-24 Paradise Road, Richmond, Surrey TW9 1SR

HOROSCOPES 2014 © Dadhichi Toth 2013

ISBN: 978 0 263 91100 8

Cover design by Anna Viniero
Typeset by Midland Typesetters

Harlequin (UK) policy is to use papers that are natural, renewable and recyclable products and made from wood grown in sustainable forests. The logging and manufacturing processes conform to the legal environmental regulations of the country of origin.

Printed and bound in Spain
by Blackprint CPI, Barcelona

Dedicated to

The Light of Intuition

Sri V. Krishnaswamy—mentor and friend

Special thanks to

Nyle Cruz for her tireless support and suggestions

Thanks to

Joram and Isaac for hanging in there

Additional appreciation to

Devika Adlakha for her excellent editorial support

ABOUT DADHICHI

Dadhichi is one of Australia's foremost astrologers and is frequently seen on television and in other media. He has the unique ability to draw from complex astrological theory to provide clear, easily understandable advice and insights for people who want to know what their futures may hold.

In the 29 years that Dadhichi has been practising astrology, face reading and other esoteric studies, he has conducted over 10,000 consultations. His clients include celebrities, political and diplomatic figures, and media and corporate identities from all over the world.

Dadhichi's unique blend of astrology and face reading helps people fulfil their true potential. His extensive experience practising Western astrology is complemented by his research into the theory and practice of Eastern forms of astrology.

Dadhichi has been a guest on many Australian television shows, and several of his political and worldwide forecasts have proved uncannily accurate. He appears regularly on Australian television networks and is a columnist for online and offline Australian publications.

His websites—www.astrology.com.au and www.facereader.com—attract hundreds of thousands of visitors each month and offer a wide variety of features, helpful information and services.

MESSAGE FROM DADHICHI

Hello once again and welcome to your 2014 horoscope!

Time and Speed are the governors of our lives these days. There's *never enough* time, and the hectic pace at which we move is getting *too much* to handle. So we oscillate between never enough and too much. We are either too slow in finishing our tasks, or the hands of the clock appear to be whizzing forward, especially when we're under pressure. We are constantly trying to create more time just to keep up with everyone else. And all those people are rushing out of control. What is this madness? We need to reclaim control of our lives and bring these terrible twins of speed and time under our control if we are ever to master our destinies.

According to Einstein and his incredible theory of relativity, speed and time are related. The faster we move, the quicker time flies. As we crank up the pace of our lives, time is impacted upon even more. You don't need me to tell you that; your experience will remind you of this fact every day, especially when you look in the mirror and see an additional wrinkle or two from time to time. Age is the favourite child of these two parents: speed and time. In the old days, it used to be the elderly who complained about the pace of time. But now, everyone, even youngsters, grumble about how little time they have and how they are forever trying to cram as much fun and experience into the moment. This attitude seems to be the order of the day, yet it will never, ever be enough.

The planets also operate on the same principle of speed and time, and this is how we generate astrological forecasts. Speed is related to the distance these planets traverse around the Sun, and the time it takes for them to do their celestial dance around the Sun is referred to as a planetary cycle.

We often talk about being in harmony with our environment and leaving as invisible a carbon footprint as we can, thus re-establishing natural equilibrium on earth. But our larger celestial environment is something we've overlooked. Ancient astrologers, however, knew the secret of our interconnectedness to the greater environment, and they gave us esoteric spiritual techniques for tuning in to these controllers of our fate. But how do you control the planets, let alone speed and time? It is through intuition, perception and self-awareness. By developing your perception and intuitive faculties, you will be one of the survivors in this brave new world.

If you're up to the challenge, this will increase your psychic abilities, thereby helping you surmount the obstacles of speed and time. You will bring yourself into harmony with your own physical, mental and emotional needs, and you will be able to tune easily in to your environment and fellow man. You will sense what these planetary energies are doing to you and can adjust yourself accordingly. This requires the subtle art of spiritual listening. This is not the hearing that is done with your ears. This is listening done with the heart. Through these simple techniques you *will* conquer time!

Our frames of reference are changing, and our ability to adapt to the light-speed pace is demanding refinements and adjustments in perception. In 2014, take the time to move at your own pace and look at what it is *you* want to achieve, not what is foisted upon you by culture, family and the establishment. Run your own race, and even if you are moving in high gear, at least you will be the one in control, not the clock. Use the transits and forecasts in the last chapter to help you gain an overview of the likely time of events. By taking control of your time and slowing the pace of life, you begin to control your destiny. In doing so, you rediscover the pleasure of your own self and the talents that you have been endowed with. This will then be a time of self-empowerment and great fulfilment.

Your astrologer,

Dadhichi Toth

CONTENTS

Libra Profile	**11**
Libra Snapshot	12
Libra Overview	15
Libra Cusps	18
Libra Celebrities	21
Libra at Large	**25**
Libra Man	26
Libra Woman	29
Libra Child	32
Libra Lover	34
Libra Friend	36
Libra Enemy	38
Libra at Home	**39**
Home Front	40
Karma, Luck and Meditation	42
Health, Wellbeing and Diet	44
Finance Finesse	46

CONTENTS
CONTINUED

Libra at Work	**47**
Libra Career	48
Libra Boss	50
Libra Employee	51
Professional Relationships: Best and Worst	52
Libra in Love	**55**
Romantic Compatibility	56
Horoscope Compatibility for Libra	58
Libra Partnerships	64
Platonic Relationships: Best and Worst	68
Sexual Relationships: Best and Worst	70
Quiz: Have You Found Your Perfect Match?	73
2014: Yearly Overview	**79**
Key Experiences	80
Romance and Friendship	81
Work and Money	84
Health, Beauty and Lifestyle	90
Karma, Spirituality and Emotional Balance	94

CONTENTS
CONTINUED

2014: Monthly and Daily Predictions	**97**
January	98
February	103
March	108
April	114
May	120
June	126
July	131
August	137
September	143
October	149
November	155
December	160
2014: Astronumerology	**167**
The Power Behind Your Name	168
Your Planetary Ruler	174
Your Planetary Forecast	175

LIBRA
PROFILE

YOU ALWAYS PASS FAILURE
ON THE WAY TO SUCCESS.

Mickey Rooney

LIBRA SNAPSHOT

Key Life Phrase		I balance
Zodiac Totem		The Scales
Zodiac Symbol		
Zodiac Facts		Seventh sign of the zodiac; movable, barren, masculine and dry
Zodiac Element		Air
Key Characteristics		Sophisticated, affable, arty, dithering, intellectual, diplomatic, thoughtful and sensitive in relationships
Compatible Star Signs		Gemini, Sagittarius, Aquarius and Leo

Mismatched Signs		Aries, Capricorn, Cancer and Taurus
Ruling Planet		Venus
Love Planets		Mars, Saturn and Uranus
Finance Planets		Mars and Pluto
Speculation Planets		Saturn and Uranus
Career Planets		Moon, Jupiter and Neptune
Spiritual and Karmic Planets		Mercury, Saturn and Uranus
Friendship Planet		Sun
Destiny Planets		Saturn and Uranus
Famous Librans		Usher, Will Smith, Zac Efron, Matt Damon, Hugh Jackman, Ryan Reynolds, Bruce Springsteen, Mario Lopez, Simon Cowell, John Lennon, Clive Owens, Gwyneth Paltrow, Naomi Watts, Christina Milian, Avril Lavigne, Gwen Stefani, Kate Winslet, Susan Sarandon, Neve Campbell, Catherine Zeta-Jones, Sharon Osbourne and Monica Bellucci

Lucky Numbers and Significant Years	5, 6, 8, 14, 15, 17, 23, 24, 26, 32, 33, 35, 41, 42, 44, 50, 51, 53, 60, 61, 69, 77, 78, 80 and 87
Lucky Gems	Clear quartz, diamond, white coral and zircon
Lucky Fragrances	Rose, geranium, clary sage, frankincense and tangerine
Affirmation/Mantra	I am harmonious in body, mind and spirit.
Lucky Days	Wednesday, Friday and Saturday

LIBRA OVERVIEW

> **EACH DAY SHOULD BE PASSED AS THOUGH IT WERE OUR LAST.**
>
> PUBLILIUS SYRUS

Driven by an acute desire for popularity, Librans are highly sociable and spirited individuals. Your quest for status and recognition opens up creative possibilities and encounters that are instrumental in carving out your destiny.

Hailing from the zodiac element of air, which governs the world of the mind, thoughts, ideas and communication, you are a born-conversationalist who bonds well with those who share intellectual interests similar to yours.

Though you thrive best among ideas, conversations and people, you ensure that it's never at the expense of your own poise and equilibrium. I've encountered many Librans who struggle to establish balance and harmony in their lives and relationships. The imbalance and chaos usually stems for your idealistic way of life. You like to see the world through rose-tinted shades, especially during your search for companions and lovers. The pursuit of balance is a key driving force in your character.

On the whole, you're a generous and gentle individual, happily sharing what you have with the ones you love. You have zero tolerance for discord or confrontations of any kind, and you prefer to stay away from anything that can negatively impact your peace of mind.

Fine Tastes

You have a proclivity for the finer things in life and you are quick to turn your nose up at anything that is substandard, mediocre or oafish.

The only perceptible flaw in the Libran personality is indecision. This is because you abhor making mistakes. As a result, you take time to do in-depth research in order to feel safe and confident as you step into the future. This may become a challenge in later years as life is bound to throw some tough decisions at you.

Though you crave popularity and recognition, you're at your best when you're being yourself, and that's what people adore you for. Unfortunately, you often doubt your own abilities and look to others for approval. There is no point in winning acceptance from the world outside. Be confident in your own skin and the rest will follow. If you want to experience self-reliance and freedom, you need to reinforce your self-confidence through continual practice. The more you believe in yourself, the greater the sense of harmony and joy in your life.

When bonding with people, you also seek inspiration from creative pursuits, and it can be rather stifling if your partner is not as intellectually or artistically gifted as you, or at least interested in these areas.

One quality Librans possess is the ability to play the skillful mediator. You are blessed with astute discernment and impartiality, which is why family and friends often rely on you to settle disputes.

Venus, your ruling planet, gives you reason to cheer. For one, it endows you with enormous charm and a splendid knack for presenting the best of yourself to the world. You dress to look glorious, and whatever the occasion, you always look fabulous and make heads turn, even without trying.

If you take the best of the aforementioned characteristics and add a dash of confidence, you'll know why Libra is often regarded as a lucky sign. People are effortlessly drawn to your innate cheerfulness and poise, and you attract a plethora of friends and well-wishers from all walks of life.

LIBRA CUSPS

ARE YOU A CUSP BABY?

Being born on the crossover of two star signs means you encompass the qualities of both. This can get tricky and sometimes you will wonder whether you're Arthur or Martha! Some of my clients are continually mystified at whether they belong to their own star sign or the one before or after. Experiencing such feelings is nothing out of ordinary. Being born on the borderline means that you take on the qualities of both signs. The following outlines show the subtle effects of these cusp dates and how they can affect your personality.

Libra–Virgo Cusp

If you were born between the 24th and the 30th of September, you are ruled by two planets—one belonging to Libra and the other to Virgo—and your character would exhibit traits from both star signs.

The combined influence of the two ruling planets, Venus and Mercury, endow you with an enormously agile and analytical mind. This makes you attentive, which can be used in both practical matters and the pursuit of spiritual insights.

As an overall rational and receptive individual, you are influenced by the critical nature of Virgo, which seeks perfection. This combined effect can be stressful for both you and others, and your mind is often in a frenzied state.

Virgos love to care and indulge while Librans are best at expressing their romantic ideals. Together, this combination benefits you greatly. After all, relationships are meant to be lived, while ideas are best thought about.

SENSITIVE AND INDECISIVE

Virgos are extremely receptive and sensitive, while Librans struggle with indecisiveness. In relationships, this may cause problems. You may find that your feelings govern your decisions, or that you overscrutinise relationships and emotions.

One critical aspect I'd like to point out is that Virgo, the sign of health, can adversely affect Libra, the sign of sociability. A stressful life is bound to have dire effects on your wellbeing. Pay keen attention to your body as it will be a perfect reflection of whether there is harmony in your life or not. Try not to be too self-critical, which is a typical Virgo tendency. Love yourself, Libra!

Libra–Scorpio Cusp

The Libra–Scorpio cusp is an intense and passionate one. If your birth date falls between the 19th and the 23rd of October, there is a high chance that Scorpio elements shape your personality.

Cusps of this combination are touted as the most sexually alluring individuals of the zodiac. On the whole, this is an electrifying union, one that endows you with socially refined elegance as well as passionate and charismatic sex appeal.

You display a prodigious flair for persuading people to satiate your desires, particularly in the bedroom, making you a phenomenal conqueror of the opposite sex. You may also exhibit commitment distress, which may be due to your upbringing or an unfavourable past, or you may be overtly critical towards loved ones. Not many realise this, but your criticisms usually stem from your devotion towards family and friends. Treat them with kid gloves, or brace yourself for some emotional clashes.

You may also have an impulsive streak, or draw conclusions that could be too overpowering for others. Indolence, not a typical Scorpio trait, could also silently creep into your lifestyle, and you will have to find ways to fight the urge to become a couch potato. On a positive note, you're gifted with strong intuitiveness and a discerning sense of judgment. You can employ these qualities to arrive at conclusions that may often elude others.

Overall, this is a phenomenal and remarkable cuspal combination, promising tranquility and harmony, as well as the Scorpionic drive to achieve all that you desire in life.

LIBRA CELEBRITIES

FAMOUS MALE: ZAC EFRON

Zac Efron was born on the 18th October, 1987, and he has no less than four planets in the sign of the Scales. Being born under Venus, the planet of love and beauty, it comes as no surprise that this famous young actor also has stunning good looks!

Having so many planets in the sign of Libra usually indicates a struggle to find equilibrium in life. Zac's increasing workload means that he needs to use this astrological trait to help him manage his schedule.

Zac's acting career began at 11 years old when he appeared in a stage production of *Gypsy*. Venus is strongly linked to the creative arts, so he would feel very comfortable performing different characters for a living. His big opportunity came with *High School Musical* (2006) for which he won the Teen Choice Award for Breakout Star. He also made cameo appearances in *CSI* and *NCIS* in 2002 and 2003. Recently, however, the films *17 Again* (2009) and *The Lucky One* (2012) have solidified his career and helped him make the transition from childhood heart-throb to serious actor.

Love is very important to Librans, but some of them find it difficult to settle down early in their life. No doubt Zac will also experience some of these challenges, particularly with his good looks. No doubt his magnetic appeal will cause him to explore as many relationships as he can before settling down.

FAMOUS FEMALE: SHARON OSBOURNE

Females born under the sign of Libra, such as Sharon Osbourne, genuinely idolise love and will do anything for their partner. This can be seen in Sharon's enduring love for bad-boy rocker Ozzy Osbourne. Most people may think that Ozzy has a screw loose, but this hasn't stopped Sharon from standing by her man, in typical Libran fashion.

Sharon was relatively unknown until she appeared in the reality TV show *The Osbournes* in 2005. The public marvelled at how she managed her role as a mother and wife in such a dysfunctional family. She is also highly regarded for her balanced Libran judgments on talkback shows and music competitions, such as *The X Factor*. Few people know that Sharon has a good head on her shoulders and that she has worked as a music promoter as well as a producer on *The Osbournes* series and other Ozzy Osbourne documentaries.

While many Librans born under the sign of the Scales struggle for balance, it appears that Sharon has achieved this objective, which is very rare. Librans are able to think through problems rationally and with a cool demeanour. By analysing life's problems and challenges in her 'Libran' way, Sharon has had a distinct advantage in getting where she is.

LIBRA
AT LARGE

WE ACCEPT THE LOVE WE
THINK WE DESERVE.

Stephen Chbosky

LIBRA MAN

LIBRA MAN: SNAPSHOT

Intellectual

Playboy

Prudent

Conversationalist

The Libran male is the epitome of charm. Ruled by the magnificent planet Venus, which endows you with an innate sense of grace and style, you inspire awe wherever you go.

The influence of Venus means that Librans are gifted with attractiveness and a charming personality from birth. Being with you can be rather addictive for others, and notwithstanding how much you adore indulgence and fame, make sure others don't advantage of you.

Librans are incapable of confrontations of any nature, and the men of this star sign are no exception. Unsurprisingly, when meaningful discussions turn into arguments, you can find a Libran male scuttling for cover. Even if you hope against hope, this trait will never change. On a happier note, the Libran man is always open to dialogue. What he dislikes is conflict, raised voices and abuse.

A Libran male likes to toy with a variety of romantic partners and is remarkably suave and debonair in his manner. Hailing from the zodiac element of air, he has a keen imagination and intellect, but he is also assailed by restlessness and wavering thoughts. This may be due to the fact that Libra is a moveable sign. As it is connected to the air, Libra is hard to bottle up and contain.

The advantageous quality of air, apart from lending a refined intellectual and artistic inclination, is that it makes you inclined towards discussions of politics, religion, human nature and relationships. This quality also reveals itself in your sharp wit and humour, which you bring to any debate or argument. At the same time, give people the opportunity to put forward their impressions before making hasty judgments.

Libran men have a remarkably intense attraction to relationships. Whether they are business or personal, relationships are your underlying motivation and inspiration.

Though independent ventures may come your way, you thrive best among people. Remember, your zodiac element is air, so you love to share ideas and talk. Although you exhibit remarkable social skills with a small group of people, you're not one to take centre stage in larger groups.

A KEEN INTELLECT

You enjoy keeping your intellect slick and sharp. You love to devour literature and stay up-to-date with current affairs. You live life to the fullest and entertain others with your life stories. Keep being yourself, Libra, as people adore you for the candour and warmth you exude.

I insinuated earlier that you're a playboy at heart, but when you finally find that special someone, you care for them unreservedly and share all that you possess. Family harmony is critical for ensuring your future happiness and joy.

The most outstanding quality you possess is your relentless pursuit to understand human nature. You're highly sensitive and perceptive, keenly aware of the unfairness and prejudices plaguing society, as well as the spiritual and philosophical anomalies that exist within it. Many Librans employ their analytical powers to seek answers that lie beyond the physical realm of this world.

You're also sexy, Libra, and like to repeatedly test the waters to ensure you're attractive and desired. This is a trait stemming from your indecisiveness, which is so intrinsic to your sign.

You are particularly finicky and demanding of the people in your life. They need to tick an array of boxes, such as grace, intellect, humour, wit and sensitivity towards the human condition. Since you love to play with ideas and make lively conversation, having friends with a similar bent will allow you to keep boredom at bay.

LIBRA WOMAN

LIBRA WOMAN: SNAPSHOT

Sexy

Cheerful

Objective

Faltering

Talkative

All Libran women are proud to hail from this star sign as it is the epitome of poise, grace and passion for life. Your effervescent Libran quality reveals itself in the vibrant energy you carry yourself with, even in times of great difficulty. Your sparkling personality, enhanced by your keen intelligence and wit, is captivating to others. You're clearly a woman of looks, charm and brains, who is also broadminded and a great conversationalist.

The Libran woman is blessed with the enviable knack of employing prudence and tactfulness in difficult circumstances, even ones that leave others scratching their heads. Being a natural mediator with unbiased judgment, you're often swift to cut through the chaos and arrive at a solution that fosters harmony and benefits everyone. This may explain why people naturally cling to you.

You're compassionate, and you happily forsake your own time and needs to support others.

FINE TASTES

You take immense pride in your taste, which reveals itself in the way you dress, your personal hygiene, the friends you pick, the way you furnish your house and the environment you live in. It also shows in your communication and the standards you set for yourself.

You can't see yourself relegated to the lowest common denominator. Mediocrity is not an option for you, and you like to set your standards high and not socialise with those of a lower class or who may sully your name. To you, integrity is paramount in your relationships.

On the whole, the greatest quest for a Libran woman is to find her ideal soul mate, the man who will sweep her off her feet. You are a hopeless dreamer, and the quest for an ideal soul mate is the most defining element of your life. When committed, you leave no stone unturned in maintaining happiness, trust and peace in your relationship. You can also get so involved that your partner's business may become a critical concern in your life as well. Remember, your presence is to help support your partner and act as cornerstone to his/her success.

You are sharp-witted and on the ball when dealing with others. Behind the perfect poise and charm is an astute mind, which is perpetually dissecting circumstances and people. This is why we come across a lot of Libran women at the helm of businesses and swathed in success and recognition. Your diplomacy allows you to blend with a wide range of people, and you're not someone who looks down on others.

You're chatty and love to entertain, and you create a haven to reflect this. People are instantly attracted to this space and are captivated by the extraordinary energy and friendship you display. You like your home to exude warmth, sophistication and grace, which are intrinsic parts of your personality.

Try to rely on yourself rather than others for your happiness. When it comes to seeking the perfect partner, your indecisiveness may create a revolving door of suitors who are unreliable and incompatible. Play the field, but don't lower your standards.

Interestingly, while balance is your key word, there will be times in your life when you struggle to achieve equilibrium. Move steadily through life and relationships, and don't let them spiral out of control. Stabilise your emotions and control your hypersensitivity as these qualities can make you dissect even innocuous statements and encounters. Instead of being a constant victim, work on your self-confidence and intuition, which you possess in abundance.

LIBRA CHILD

As the parent of a Libran child, you need to engage in constant communication, as they respond best to open dialogue. From the moment your Libran offspring comes into this world, he or she is naturally endowed with inquisitiveness and a keen intellect. This may prove to be a challenge, but if you foster this quality in your child, you will witness them blossom into wonderful adults.

The second factor critical to raising a happy Libran child is creating a peaceful and harmonious domestic atmosphere. Though this holds true for all children, it is particularly important for Libran children. If you've leafed through the preceding pages, you will know by now that Librans are averse to confrontation, temper outbursts and even raised voices. If you happen to be experiencing discord or divorce, my advice would be to pay keen attention to your little one. If you provide comfort and assurance through dialogue, the transition will be seamless. Your child will respond best to reasoning, which means that talking it out will mitigate their stress levels under such circumstances.

As Libran children grow, they will turn into wonderfully social beings, lively and forever seeking harmony among friendships. If you notice them trying too hard to win friends, teach them to accept themselves for who they are and not change themselves to win acceptance from others. Tell them that the right friends will come into their life at the right time, and that they need to be themselves for that to happen.

If you are a working parent, try not to leave your child unaccompanied in your absence. Libran children abhor isolation or being cut off from channels of communication. When both parents work, organise for a babysitter, friend or family member to drop by for a while even when the child is old enough to be safely left alone. This will make a huge difference in the long run.

> ## Sporty Libra
>
> Games and sports offer the perfect outlet for their imagination and mental energies. Strategic games like tennis and soccer, as well as gymnastics, dance and the other creative arts, can direct your child's energies in a constructive way.

Libran children can be hypersensitive, and they may react to your innocuously insensitive or casual remarks. If you happen to catch them sulking, instead of letting them be, swiftly take action by correcting your statement or clarifying what you intended. You'll have to teach them the art of developing a thick skin in order to calmly deal with the world around them as they grow older.

An empty mind is the devil's workshop, and this is very much the case with Libran children. Because of their highly developed intellectual abilities, they're naturally studious, and it's imperative to surround them with ample ways to exercise their minds and hands. They should also do extremely well at school, particularly in subjects such as art, culture and literature. By making these subjects a part of their educational regime, you will enable them to harness their natural abilities.

LIBRA LOVER

> SO LONG AS WE ARE LOVED BY OTHERS,
> I SHOULD SAY THAT WE ARE ALMOST INDISPENSABLE;
> AND NO MAN IS USELESS WHILE HE HAS A FRIEND.
>
> ROBERT LOUIS STEVENSON

Ruled by the planet Venus, you're the eternal lover and the most loveable star sign of the zodiac. You respond instinctively to love and are enamoured by the concept of romance from an early age.

Your finest quality is your propensity to see the goodness in others, especially the ones you love. Regardless of the circumstances, you aim to appreciate and admire your significant other. This may not be a simple affair as your high standards can make you very demanding. This may be one of the reasons why a majority of Libran men like to play the field before surrendering their hearts to their chosen one.

Indecisive Libra

Even if you do toy with several close and seemingly promising relationships, you may find yourself having to choose between two or more lovers. Add to this the inherent indecisiveness that is your lifelong companion, and you have the reason why commitment may elude you.

As mentioned, you are an expert at setting astronomical standards, making it excruciatingly hard both for yourself and the person you love. This may put people on such a high pedestal that you refuse to believe they're only human when they fail.

Love consumes the majority of your attention and reveals itself in a burgeoning family life, a content spouse and children that you dote upon. To you, nothing is more important than this. At the same time, do not forget to rejuvenate your soul by seeking space and independence, as well as conversations with a diverse mix of people and temperaments. To this end, your choice of partner is pivotal. You need someone who is sensitive and understanding about your need for space. You're not someone who allows others to tie them down and smother their social and intellectual life. This would be a recipe for disaster.

In matters of love, take your time to weigh all possibilities before taking the plunge. At the same time, Libra, try to loosen up and forgive other people's shortcomings.

You seek a partner with grace, style, intellect, dedication and wit. You expect them to display greater or similar fervour and enthusiasm for life. Settling down with a reticent individual may not be a good idea as you grow best in an environment with constant dialogue in which you communicate your fears, feelings, joys and hope for building a life together.

On the whole, you're a fantastic lover, except that your wavering mind and idealistic romanticism may often undermine the thing you cherish so deeply. If you relax and accept others for who they are, Libra, you're set to go!

LIBRA FRIEND

In my many years as an astrologer, I am yet to encounter a Libran who isn't compassionate or impartial. You're the eternal peacemaker, and what better way to show this than through the care and objectivity with which you deal with yourself and others.

SWEET-TEMPERED AND LOVABLE

The influence of Venus makes you sweet-tempered and lovable, and you shine best with family and friends. Wherever you go, you enliven the mood with your spirit and fervour.

Librans are great storytellers, but they're equally adept at listening. Not only do they listen to your tales, they have an incredible knack for helping you view life from an unbiased perspective. Come rain or shine, one can bank on your Libran friend for sane advice.

Your Libran friends have a tendency to surpass themselves in their attempt to win acceptance from others. This acute desire to please may leave you feeling displeased and frustrated, especially when you are asking them for advice on a decision. At such moments, Libra may be evasive and indecisive, as they don't want to offend others or hurt their feelings.

Librans are oblivious to the strata of society that others come from, and they can happily engage with people of any culture or class. Though uncompromising in their standards, they never look down on those of an inferior status. Unconcerned with material pleasures, they genuinely care about their loved ones and endeavour to connect with the spiritual aspect of another human being.

Since they are hugely devoted to nurturing and loving, whether it's a relative, colleague, neighbour or friend, Librans always strive to enhance their relationships and create harmony around them. The primary reason for this is because Librans detest solitude of any kind. However, being alone is not the same as being lonely. This is why I always advise my Libran friends and clients to foster a relationship with themselves before they build a castle with the people they love.

Because Librans are attractive, they're also understandably popular. This may go too far when fascination turns into obsession, or when they fuss over being at their fashionable best.

One thing to remember is that Librans avoid conflict like the plague. When you desire peace or reconciliation, you might wind up exasperated with your Libran friend, who walks away from negative conversations and refuses to address your grievances. In this situation, calm reasoning and dialogue is the only language they respond to.

LIBRA ENEMY

> **PEACE CANNOT BE KEPT BY FORCE. IT CAN ONLY BE ACHIEVED BY UNDERSTANDING.**
> ALBERT EINSTEIN

I can't help but be amused at the thought of Libran enemies. Ever spotted a sheep in the fields, only to discover that it was a wolf? That's exactly how I would describe Libran enemies—as wolves in sheep's clothing.

They are adept at being tactful and diplomatic, and they often leave you wondering whether they're irked or not. They're born with a sense of grace, calm and balance, and even when they're seething from within, it can be tricky to ascertain the degree of their anger, resentment or fury.

Don't get swayed by their calm and collected temperament. If a Libran loses their cool, they can rip you apart in ways that may leave you hurting for a long time. They can erupt suddenly and verbally massacre you, knowing exactly where it hurts. Try not to venture into such a zone or scenario. Since Librans avoid confrontations, you can imagine how much rage it would take to push them to the edge.

LIBRA
AT HOME

EMPTY POCKETS NEVER HELD ANYONE BACK. ONLY EMPTY HEADS AND EMPTY HEARTS CAN DO THAT.

Norman Vincent Peale

HOME FRONT

Although Librans are primarily social butterflies, family assumes great significance in their lives. In fact they're almost obsessed with relationships and creating a loving and comfortable domestic haven for their loved ones.

Stimulated by Venus, you seek attractiveness in the way you look, speak and move, but also in everything around you. This explains your penchant for exclusive and opulent things. However, you're intrinsically artistic, and even if you may not have the luxury of wealth, you can still brighten up a space in a manner that is appealing, elegant and aesthetically pleasing for everyone.

The furnishings, artwork and designs in a Libran home express your creative flair and preferred colour palette. You blend colours seamlessly, preferring rich tones of white and cream, as well as light sandy or autumn shades. Your paintings may possess a dash of red or black to contrast boldly with these subdued colors. Since you like to unwind in a zone of warmth and ease, you create a home that is both elegant and practical. Some Librans may also have old-fashioned tastes, which is why they prefer lace, wrought iron and intricately designed glasses to express their personality.

Libra, you need to create enough space in your home to entertain. This is extremely important for keeping you fulfilled as a person. You love having family and friends over and may even use a part of your house as a study area. This will keep you in touch with people, conversations and intellectual endeavour at all times. It may also be your secret place to retire, allowing you to gather your thoughts and let your artistic imagination run wild.

Ornamentation may also characterise a Libran home. This includes photo frames, works of art, fragrant candles with exquisite candlesticks, mirrors and even pottery in various shapes, colours and sizes. The Libran home is more than just a comfortable living space. In extreme cases it can be as good as a well stocked museum, making it a must for family and friends!

KARMA, LUCK AND MEDITATION

Libra, you're blessed with an incredible ability to communicate and understand human nature. This is because Gemini is in your past karma star sign, which makes you good at establishing an excellent rapport with those around you.

Your past karma and good fortune are also influenced by the providential planet Mercury, which is quick-moving by nature. Because of this mobile characteristic, your actions are quick to bear fruit, and the results often work in your favour.

Aquarius and its ruler, Uranus, govern your future karma and what lies in store for you. Uranus is liberal, forward-moving, stimulating and exhilarating, which signals a fascinating future with phases that enhance your growth and invigorate your inherent wisdom.

Your life phrase is 'I balance', but your ficklemindedness and wavering thought processes may challenge this. The onus is on you to work your way out of this and judge how you can weigh up the relationships around you.

Friday, Saturday and Wednesday are the best days for self-advancement, meditation and spiritual pursuits. Regardless of how deeply you cherish your loved ones, set aside some time for personal revitalisation, which will give you peace and inner poise.

Lucky Days

Your luckiest days are Wednesday, Friday and Saturday.

Lucky Numbers

Lucky numbers for Libra include the following. You may wish to experiment with these in Lotto and other games of chance.

6, 15, 24, 33, 42, 51

5, 14, 23, 32, 41, 50

8, 17, 26, 35, 44, 53

Destiny Years

The most significant years in your life are likely to be 5, 6, 8, 14, 15, 17, 23, 24, 26, 32, 33, 35, 41, 42, 44, 50, 51, 53, 60, 61, 69, 77, 78, 80 and 87.

HEALTH, WELLBEING AND DIET

Past experience tells me that most air signs, including Libra, are slender in frame and physically alluring. Of course, exceptions abound, but due to the influence of Venus, Libran women display particular charm and grace. They also have beautiful, voluptuous bodies, although they are not usually overweight.

Though you are blessed with favourable health, Libra, you must guard against the influence of Venus, which could push you into overdoing things at the cost of your own wellbeing. Be wary of your love for pleasure, gluttony and lack of sleep, as these are bound to impact on your health. Taurus is similar to you when it comes to matters of health as they, too, are ruled by Venus. Exercise moderation, Libra.

You might want to be kinder towards your kidneys and urinary tract, as they are constitutionally weak. According to Chinese medicine, the kidneys feed the life force to other internal organs. Abundant water intake, minimal fast food and avoiding overcooked food will help bolster your overall health.

I have encountered many Librans who are constant victims of headaches and migraines. Libra, you must understand how critical sleep, diet and mental balance are for you. Making yourself physically exhausted due to lack of sleep or overanalysis will pose a definite threat to your health. Yoga or deep breathing techniques can provide much-needed respite.

Libra, you will gain more benefit from a diet that is rich in fresh fruits and glistening green vegetables rather than milk, icecream or cheese. Whole grains are an obvious blessing, but ensure that you do not overdo the starch quotient in your body through breads, biscuits or other pastries.

✾ FINANCE FINESSE ✾

Libra, you are a stickler for luxury and opulence, and your high standards outshine what most people desire in life. In fact, you are orgasmically turned on by money and riches as they give you the ability to royally indulge your Libran pursuits.

From an astrological point of view, Scorpio and the ruling planets of Pluto and Mars form immunity over the way you earn money, while Virgo and Mercury determine how you consume it. This bestows on you the incredible ability to be frugal as well as squander money according to your whims!

Because you prefer to live large, you glam up your parties with a staggering amount of lavishness and abundance, and you splurge a lot more than you need to. You also demand and bestow glamorous gifts due to your inherent generosity and love. But bear in mind that you need to secure your own future by conserving rather than thoughtlessly spending.

As mentioned earlier, the idea of balance needs keen attention and constant application. Instead of trying to impress everyone, work on ways to balance your finances and use money wisely. It's a Libran tendency to go out of their way to impress others, but you need to be judicious in matters of finances, or all that security will disappear before you get a chance to enjoy it.

LIBRA
AT WORK

PERFORM EVERY ACT IN LIFE
AS IF IT WERE YOUR LAST.

Marcus Aurelius

LIBRA CAREER

IDEAL PROFESSIONS

Public Relations

Sales Consultant Designer

Interior Decorator

Artist

Architect

Libra, you have remarkable qualities that make you outshine others in any workplace, business or professional endeavour. Cutting corners is not your style, and sometimes you may be mistaken for a Virgo! Like Virgo, you are a perfectionist in all that you do. You prefer working unhurriedly rather than racing around to produce a half-hearted result.

Many Librans who aspire to positions of authority find it difficult to make the leap because of their extreme attachment to friends and co-workers. Even if you happen to get there, you may find yourself grappling with your inability to exert professional weight over your colleagues. Loosen up, Libra, and don't think about it so much. We're all playing our parts, so unwind and take it easy!

You make a great professional, Libra. Not only are you responsive, pleasant and cheerful, but you also work with creative and persistent effort to bring a task to fruition. At the same time, your tendency to be overfriendly can complicate things and distract you from focusing on yourself. Keep a tab on the hours you work and the socialising you do.

PUBLIC RELATIONS DYNAMO

Libra is often touted as the public relations zone of the zodiac, which signals a natural flair for people of all temperaments, as well as the ability to shine in sales, marketing or spirituality. In short, as long as you are in a work environment that encourages you to express yourself and engage in meaningful work, success and joy will be yours.

Evenhandedness, integrity and impartiality form the heart of your work ethic, and anyone who works with you knows this. At the same time, being too idealistic is not always wise. You are bound to encounter people who take advantage of your sincerity and work against your best interests.

The Moon, which is alterable and variable by nature, also happens to be your career planet. This means that you will find yourself seeking diversity and change, which may throw your career a little off track, but if you focus on the present rather than the future, the discontent will wane and you will be a lot happier.

I can see indecisiveness rear its ugly head this year, and such vacillation is bound to have an adverse effect on your ability to climb up the career ladder and be more ruthless in business. Since you're so inept at handling confrontations, you'll find yourself taking the easy way out rather than decisively take charge, even when situations demand it.

LIBRA BOSS

If you have a Libran boss, you'll be amazed at the swiftness with which they can accomplish a task, even when faced with tight deadlines. They are the epitome of multi-tasking, and they display streaks similar to those of Gemini and Virgo when it comes to perfection and the successful management of a project.

Your Libran boss is intelligent, clever and gifted. As the saying goes, they could sell ice to the Eskimos! They have a knack for impressing and convincing people, and with their unbiased view, they are a blessing indeed. However, this unprejudiced approach makes it difficult for those want to curry favour with them.

Libran bosses falter only when it comes to decision-making. Astrologically speaking, air signs can be predominantly intellectual by nature. Unsurprisingly, you Libran boss will be forever analysing and collating notes. This quality can be either advantageous or detrimental when it comes to making decisions. They eventually reach a conclusion, but they take longer to get there than most.

Libran bosses are fairly progressive because Aquarius is the other air sign in the Zodiac triangle. This makes their minds swift, astute, forward-thinking and endowed with eclectic tastes. All in all, you can consider yourself fortunate if you're born under the sign of the Scales.

LIBRA EMPLOYEE

Employing a Libran brings an element of attractiveness and confidence to the workplace, and they are the best face to represent a company or department. You may first notice their immaculate clothing, manicured nails and sparkling footwear before being swept away by their innate charm and poise.

A Libran employee is receptive, sharp and adept at juggling many tasks at the same time. Just like the air, which is forever in motion, the Libran employee seeks diversity and creative independence to give their best.

At the same time, they have highly evolved and agile minds and are ideally suited to jobs that require human interactions, such as issue resolution and negotiation. Placing them in such a position in the workplace will help you get the best from Libran employees.

You, Libra, like to create the perfect ambience to exploit your energy in the most optimum manner and, being creative at heart, you're not someone who allows much interference. Although this may allow you to produce some remarkable work, your relationship with your colleagues may suffer.

> ### *Be Mindful of Others*
>
> In your creative intensity, you may inadvertently offend others by dismissing their ideas. Remember, 'I balance' is your life phrase, and it's imperative that you apply this when you deal with co-workers.

You constantly seek mental stimulation, and if you're working in an atmosphere with people who are graceful and respectful of your creative and intellectual skills, the sky's the limit.

PROFESSIONAL RELATIONSHIPS: BEST AND WORST

BEST PAIRING: LIBRA AND LIBRA

This pairing rates highly because you are both star twins. The element that determines success or failure in a business venture is the relationship between the partners involved. While you both enjoy phenomenal clarity and trust, decision-making is not your forte. This is possibly the greatest weakness in your partnership, which may ultimately cause your relationship to fall apart.

On a happy note, you both love being surrounded by people and are genuinely so affable that you can foster a long-lasting friendship and bring joy and excitement to a business venture. At the same time, you may chafe the thin line between business and pleasure and find yourself unable to communicate on a professional level. I'd suggest that you hold on to such closeness until you both feel stable with the venture and enjoy a sufficient inflow of cash.

Though you're skilled at multitasking, grappling with more than you can handle may affect your relationship. And in your attempt to win acceptance from the world, you may get distracted from the essentials of your business enterprise. Perhaps you could try swapping positions to ensure that one of you remains squarely focused while the other pursues opportunities and meetings.

As you are both social butterflies, you will have a packed social calendar, which will make your business life frenzied. Commitment to family and friends is admirable, but not when it impinges on the success of your business. Address these concerns at the nascent stages of your professional venture, Libra.

You both respond positively to carefully laid out plans. When you have these in place, you will have the ideal foundation to begin your professional journey.

WORST PAIRING: LIBRA AND CANCER

Even though Cancer falls in the career sector of your Zodiac, take my advice and try to maneuver out of this association. While you are instantly attracted to Cancer's strength and resilience, you remain hopelessly oblivious to their inherent sensitivity and sullenness, which they closely guard. With time, however, the cracks become visible and manifest as extreme moodiness and protectiveness, which are traits that can rip your sanity apart. Their temperamental outbursts, punctured by your indecisiveness, can create mayhem and disharmony.

Being an air sign, you are naturally endowed with a rational and investigative outlook to solving problems, both professionally and personally. Though an asset, this quality is rendered useless when teamed with your Cancerian associate's reliance on their gut instinct. While you painstakingly ensure that all aspects of your business are accounted for and logically worked out, Cancer's intuitiveness will not rate in your books. This creates friction that affects every phase of your work.

A POOR MATCH

A small semblance of harmony may reveal itself when Cancer cares for and nurtures your imaginative instincts, but you would rather have them pour this commitment into profitable business results and solidifying the client base.

On the whole, notwithstanding the few commonalities you share, you both have different expectations from each other, and this combination will bring stress, chaos and mistrust. Approach this venture with considerable caution, Libra.

LIBRA
IN LOVE

THE ONLY PEOPLE FOR ME ARE THE MAD ONES, THE ONES WHO ARE MAD TO LIVE, MAD TO TALK, MAD TO BE SAVED, DESIROUS OF EVERYTHING AT THE SAME TIME, THE ONES WHO NEVER YAWN OR SAY A COMMONPLACE THING, BUT BURN, BURN, BURN.

Jack Kerouac

ROMANTIC COMPATIBILITY

Are you compatible with your current partner, lover or friend? Astrology reveals a great deal about people and their relationships through their star signs. In this chapter, I'd like to show you how to better appreciate your strengths and challenges using Sun sign compatibility.

The Sun reflects your drive, willpower and personality. The essential qualities of two star signs blend like two pure colours producing an entirely new colour. Relationships, similarly, produce their own emotional colours when two people interact. The following is a general guide to your romantic prospects with others and how, by knowing the astrological 'colour' of each other, the art of love can help you create a masterpiece.

The Star Sign Compatibility for Love and Friendship table rates your chance as a percentage of general compatibility, while the Horoscope Compatibility table summarises the reasons why. Each star sign combination is followed by the elements of those star signs and the result of their combining. For instance, Aries is a fire sign and Aquarius is an air sign and this combination produces a lot of 'hot air'. Air feeds fire and fire warms air. In fact, fire requires air. However, not all air and fire combinations work.

When reading the following, I ask you to remember that no two star signs are ever *totally* incompatible. With effort and compromise, even the most 'difficult' astrological matches can work. Don't close your mind to the full range of life's possibilities! Learning about each other and us is the most important facet of astrology.

Good luck in your search for love, and may the stars shine upon you in 2014!

STAR SIGN COMPATIBILITY FOR LOVE AND FRIENDSHIP (PERCENTAGES)

	Aries	Taurus	Gemini	Cancer	Leo	Virgo	Libra	Scorpio	Sagittarius	Capricorn	Aquarius	Pisces
Aries	60	65	65	65	90	45	70	80	90	50	55	65
Taurus	60	70	70	80	70	90	75	85	50	95	80	85
Gemini	70	70	75	60	80	75	90	60	75	50	90	50
Cancer	65	80	60	75	70	75	60	95	55	45	70	90
Leo	90	70	80	70	85	75	65	75	95	45	70	75
Virgo	45	90	75	75	75	70	80	85	70	95	50	70
Libra	70	75	90	60	65	80	80	85	80	85	95	50
Scorpio	80	85	60	95	75	85	85	90	80	65	60	95
Sagittarius	90	50	75	55	95	70	80	85	85	55	60	75
Capricorn	50	95	50	45	45	95	85	65	55	85	70	85
Aquarius	55	80	90	70	70	50	95	60	60	70	80	55
Pisces	65	85	50	90	75	70	50	95	75	85	55	80

HOROSCOPE COMPATIBILITY FOR LIBRA

Libra with		Romance/Sexual
Aries		Opposites often attract, but in this case they don't!
Taurus		Sporadic passion and temperamental mood swings
Gemini		A spectacular union; the emotional and intellectual bonding translates into playful and inventive lovemaking
Cancer		Electrifying initially, but will wane with time; Cancer's lack of communication and mood swings can be hugely taxing

	Friendship		Professional
✔	Inspiring and stimulating	✔	A good business partnership provided you yield to Aries
✘	Your social life is lively and full; grounded and homely Taurus offers a comfortable and peaceful space to connect	✔	Taurus is endowed with astute financial prowess that could add a lot to the business; allow trust to flow in for optimal results
✔	A fantastic friendship with common vision, style and emotional compatibility	✔	You can be a force to reckon with in the professional sphere; your intellect and analytical minds signal profitability in all ventures
✔	Satisfactory association overall; a little effort and endurance will ensure peace and harmony with Cancer	✘	Cancer brings a lot of creativity and ingenuity to the business, but you desire more stability than what they can offer

Libra with		Romance/Sexual
Leo		A first rate combination; your warmth and love invigorates Leo's fiery disposition
Virgo		Sexually intriguing, even though Virgo can be fanatical about hygiene or schedules
Libra		A gentle and passionate union, though you may be too preoccupied with social engagements
Scorpio		Scorpio is the sexiest sign of the zodiac, and apart from their appeal, there's a lot that you admire about them; a dynamic and promising union
Sagittarius		A fabulous combination that is fiery in the bedroom as well as emotionally soothing

	Friendship		Professional
✔	Take time to tune into Leo and you'll be pleased at the commonalities you share	✔	Financially remarkable and rewarding; there's a lot Leo can do to ensure the triumph of a venture
✘	You set your standards high, but Virgo goes further! They can be extremely demanding, and even your best may not be good enough	✔	You both bring your best to this partnership; make Virgo the accountant or administrator while you, Libra, do the public relations
✔	You are both Zodiac twins, and with so much in common, exciting times are set to roll!	✔	Too much socialising destabilises your business, and with your collective and inherent indecisiveness, this may not be the best match
✔	They captivate you with their philosophies, intellect, wit and humour, and you both enjoy relaxed and fun-loving communication	✔	A promising combination; they're as gifted and as dedicated as you are, Libra
✔	A gratifying, exciting and passionate friendship; brace yourself for some amazing travel escapades	✘	Socialising and adventure may distract you from serious business; you need discipline to get the best out of this union

Libra with		Romance/Sexual
Capricorn	💔	Deep-thinking Capricorn needs a lot of prodding, but with time and patience it can be a rewarding partnership
Aquarius	🔥❤	Exciting and thrilling romantic association, with imaginative lovemaking
Pisces	❤	A satisfactory spiritual combination, though not your cup of tea, either emotionally or physically

	Friendship		Professional
✗	A natural friendship will evolve with time; Capricorn moves slowly and cautiously	✓	You make excellent business partners, and you'll both enjoy financial and professional rewards
✓	A pleasant and friendly connection with a passionate and stimulating rapport	✗	Aquarius prefers to be unconventional, so you may have to adapt to make your business alliance work
✗	Highly mismatched due to the water versus air element; requires painstaking effort for it to work	✗	A bit of friction as Pisces goes with their gut while you like to be analytical; if you can trust in their intuition, this partnership could work

LIBRA IN LOVE | 63

LIBRA PARTNERSHIPS

Libra + Aries

Aries is clear-thinking, while you're perpetually uncertain. The best approach is for you to hand over the responsibility and devote yourself to what you do best. Remember, this fire and air combination can be fiery, zesty and exciting, and chances of this relationship working are fairly high.

Libra + Taurus

The combination of air and earth is bound to rake up a dust storm. Need I say more, Libra? Although you share your ruling planet, Venus, the dissimilarities in your star signs outweigh the commonalities.

Libra + Gemini

This is a hugely rewarding and satisfying relationship on all levels. Because the two of you are communicative and emotionally compatible, everything else falls into place. A big thumbs up!

Libra + Cancer

An exciting relationship at the start as you are feminine and masculine signs of the zodiac and sensitive to each other's needs. However, you both have erratic temperaments and can be unstable and uncommunicative, which will negatively impact on your bond.

Libra + Leo

From the looks of it, this is an exceptional partnership. The two of you share instant romantic chemistry, enjoy social engagements, love being surrounded by people and make great listeners and friends. What more could you hope for?

Libra + Virgo

Libra, you like to plan and design, but in a fairly relaxed manner, unlike the fanatical Virgo, who swears by norms and schedules. Chances of this association working are fair to middling.

Libra + Libra

A remarkable combination, even though your packed social calendars may distract you from giving attention to each other. Invest quality time in making the relationship work.

Libra + Scorpio

You're enthralled by Scorpio's mental agility and their high sex appeal. You both share an immense emotional and intellectual bond, making this a promising relationship for both of you.

Libra + Sagittarius

Sagittarius is forthright and occasionally thorny for you, Libra. You prefer gracefulness in conversations. But if you overlook their shortcomings, this can be a strong relationship.

Libra + Capricorn

Overall, your individual star signs are comfortable and friendly, but you need to work hard at drawing your Capricorn partner out of their intense disposition. While you may have a slow start, this relationship has the potential to mature like a beautiful wine.

Libra + Aquarius

This relationship is an absolute joy ride, though it can be unpredictable at times. You're fascinated by Aquarius's progressiveness, and apart from minor irregularities, adventure and fun form a part of this union.

Libra + Pisces

An absolute downer. You stand at cross purposes with one another, and whilst Pisces likes to dream, you prefer to think. You may often find them in their own world, entirely detached from your thought processes. You also have different approaches to friendship and life.

PLATONIC RELATIONSHIPS: BEST AND WORST

BEST PAIRING: LIBRA AND SAGITTARIUS

Air and fire are a perfect fit, which is why this association is one of the best for platonic connection. The fire sign of Sagittarius is gregarious, outgoing and tender when it comes to friendship and love.

Although your respective ruling planets, Venus and Jupiter, are not astrologically friendly, they generate significant good fortune when they combine. This helps bolster the friendship you both share.

Libra desires communication in all areas, and there is no one better than Sagittarius, who is gifted with immense flair and forthrightness in their communication style. When picking friends, Libra, you set very high standards, and you respect Sagittarius for the experience, intellect and sound philosophical views they bring to a relationship.

Another Sagittarian quality you admire is their love for people. Both of you want an active social life with family and friends, and this commonality offers the perfect platform for a lasting friendship. Because Sagittarius loves adventure and travel, the idea of exploring the world and encountering new people and cultures is something that will consolidate your friendship even further.

Because you abhor confrontation, Libra, you need a patient ear in times of distress. Again, your Sagittarian friend will give you ample opportunity to express all that bottled up venom. They're easygoing and manage to sooth your otherwise frenzied nerves. Sagittarius is a best friend who never judges and who makes you feel confident.

WORST PAIRING: LIBRA AND ARIES

Libra and Aries are known to attract one another with magnetising fury, and from my own understanding, the attraction can be quite intense, at least at the beginning. But if you hang in there a little longer, you'll soon encounter the fiery nature of Aries, which is decisive, upfront and often intimidating.

Your indecisiveness can be a real turn off for them, and although you strive to be civil towards each other, you will not be able to ignore the underlying stress lurking in the friendship

---

DOMINANT ARIES

Libra, you're far more graceful in your etiquette and communication, and you are often let down by Aries' constant attempts to upstage you. Aries is just as sociable as you, but you are likely to be dominated and tossed around by them.

Interestingly, you inspire Aries with your Libran quality of air, and they blaze brightly in your presence. You may take a while to realise it, but Aries has little regard for your needs, which makes this association a one-way street.

SEXUAL RELATIONSHIPS: BEST AND WORST

BEST PAIRING: LIBRA AND AQUARIUS

Aquarius hails from the same zodiac element as you, Libra. Air signs are blessed with intellect, communicativeness and the ability to generate ideas. This makes the two of you a force to be reckoned with, and it is also a sexual match that I consider to be one of the best.

You are fascinated by the effervescence, spontaneity and wit that are fundamental to the character of Aquarius, and on a more profound level, you also have a high regard for their ability to think outside conventional boundaries and translate their ideas and concepts into social and global reform. Subjects such as politics, philosophy and religion interest them greatly, and since you are devoted to these areas, you have a strong foundation for emotional bonding. At the same time, they also admire your sociability, communicativeness, imagination, style and attractiveness.

This basis makes it easy for you to connect with an Aquarian on all levels, and the chemistry you share has the potential to transform into an intimate and passionate sexual relationship. Secretly, you both enjoy an unconventional approach to lovemaking as well.

Security and Fulfilment

You're a flirt at heart, Libra, and like you, Aquarians prefer to play around before committing to a lifelong partner. Your first connection is intellectual, but it later becomes emotional and physical. When it comes to security and fulfilment on an intimate level, your search begins and ends with Aquarius.

All of this makes Aquarius your perfect partner. Commitment may be elusive at the start of your association, but once you both comprehend how intensely compatible you are, you'll be more than eager to take the plunge. Boredom doesn't exist in your relationship as you will have a knack for stimulating each other's imagination and creating something wonderful and awe-inspiring.

WORST PAIRING: LIBRA AND PISCES

The dissimilarity between you and Pisces makes me question your inclination to go down this path. Though your ruling planet, Venus, is illustrious and glorified due to the influence of Pisces, this may have more to do with the altruistic streak you both possess rather than physical attraction.

Though Pisces' selflessness may charm you initially, you may have a hard time comprehending the way they respond to others, their style of communication, the reason they behave as they do.

Pisces are eternal dreamers, and even though they may be good listeners, they can disappear into their thoughts and appear clueless at the end. This makes you feel disrespected and disconnected from them. Librans demand absolute awareness and attention from their partners, and such tacit disengagement can be ascribed to their meditative state of mind. Clearly, this is not your cup of tea, Libra.

Pisces is not quite as social as you are, and like their Cancerian cousins, they can be moody and temperamental. When it comes to addressing relationship issues, they may choose to bottle up their feelings and sulk, while you prefer two-way communication. This can get in the way of your emotional bonding and stifle your physical relationship as well.

Pisces floats in the realm of feelings and intuitive responses to life. This is anathema to Libra's intellectual and analytical approach to life and relationships. At best, you can maintain a cordial relationship with your Pisces friend. Don't fall into the romance trap. Your chances of romantic success with Pisces are abysmally low.

QUIZ: HAVE YOU FOUND YOUR PERFECT MATCH?

Do you dare take the following quiz to see how good a lover you are? Remember, although the truth sometimes hurts, it's the only way to develop your relationship skills.

We are all searching for our soul mate: that idyllic romantic partner who will fulfil our wildest dreams of love and emotional security. Unfortunately, finding true love isn't easy. Sometimes, even when you are in a relationship, you can't help but wonder whether or not your partner is right for you. How can you possibly know?

It's essential to question your relationships and work on ways to improve your communication and overall happiness. When meeting someone new, it's also a good idea to study their intentions and read between the lines. In the first instance, when your hormones are taking over, it's easy to get carried away and forget some of the basic principles of what makes a relationship endure.

You're probably wondering where to start. Are you in a relationship at the moment? Are you looking for love but finding it difficult to choose between two or more people? Are you simply not able to meet someone at all? Well, there are some basic questions you can ask yourself to discover how suited you and your partner are. And if you don't have a partner, consider your previous relationships to improve your chances next time.

The following quiz is a serious attempt to take an honest look at yourself and see whether or not your relationships are on track. Don't rush through this questionnaire. Think carefully about your practical day-to-day life and whether or not the relationship you are in genuinely fulfils your needs and the other person's needs. There's no point being in a relationship if you're gaining no satisfaction out of it.

Now, if you aren't completely satisfied with the results you get, don't give up! It's an opportunity for you to work on the relationship and improve things. But you mustn't let your ego get in the way as that's not going to get you anywhere.

Born lovers, Librans cherish relationships and want their partners to dote upon them at all times. Love assumes the spotlight in your life, and taking into consideration your indecisiveness and idealism in relationships, it's imperative that you make the right choice to last a lifetime. Below is your checklist, Libra, to see if he or she is the right one for you.

Scoring System:

Yes = 1 point

No = 0 points

- ❓ Does she/he appreciate and admire you, and are they vocal about it?
- ❓ Does she/he like to spend ample time with you?
- ❓ Does she/he enjoy holding your hand in public?
- ❓ Does she/he sweep you off your feet, or wish to move mountains for you?
- ❓ Is she/he humorous and easygoing?
- ❓ Does she/he always remember anniversaries?
- ❓ Does she/he often surprise you with sweet gestures and thoughtful gifts?
- ❓ Does she/he believe in togetherness, especially on vacation?
- ❓ Is she/he graceful and refined, never embarrassing you in public or private?
- ❓ Is she/he patient enough to wait until you make a decision?
- ❓ Is she/he sensitive about giving you ample time to dress for an outing?
- ❓ Does she/he enjoy intimacy, and is she/he daring in the bedroom?
- ❓ Does she/he give you space when you need it the most?

- ❓ Does she/he love to talk, listen and share, sometimes into the night, and cuddling during breaks?

- ❓ Does she/he stimulate you mentally, emotionally, intellectually, sexually and spiritually?

- ❓ Do you feel balanced, content and in sync in your relationship?

Have you jotted down your answers honestly? If you're finding it hard to come up with the right answers, let your intuition help you, and try not to force the answer. Of course there's no point in turning a blind eye to treatment that is less than acceptable, otherwise you're not going to have a realistic appraisal of your prospects with your current love interest. Here are the possible points you can score:

8 to 16

A good match. This shows that you and your partner enjoy a healthy understanding and reciprocate just the way you need. However, this is no reason to be slack out of complacency. You must continue working and improving your bond to make it shine more brilliantly than it does now.

5 to 7

Half-hearted prospect. You need to work hard at building your relationship and engage in honest self-examination. It takes two to tango, so you're obviously aware that you are both to blame. Go through each question systematically, making notes of areas where you can improve yourself. Undertaking this self-examination will guarantee favourable shifts in your relationship. But if things don't improve in spite of the effort, it may be time for you to rethink your future with this person.

0 to 4

On the rocks. I'm sorry to say that this relationship is completely devoid of basic mutual respect and understanding. It's likely that the two of you argue a lot. Your partner is also completely oblivious to your emotional needs. This is the perfect example of incompatibility. The big question is: Why are you still with this person? This requires some brutally honest self-examination on your part. You need to see whether there is some inherent insecurity within you that is causing you to hold onto something that has outgrown its use in your life. You may also be a victim of fear, which is preventing you from letting go of a relationship that no longer fulfils your needs. Self-honesty is the key here. You need to make some rather bold sacrifices to attract the right partner into your life.

2014
YEARLY OVERVIEW

TIME IS FREE, BUT IT'S PRICELESS. YOU CAN'T OWN IT, BUT YOU CAN USE IT. YOU CAN'T KEEP IT, BUT YOU CAN SPEND IT. ONCE YOU'VE LOST IT, YOU CAN NEVER GET IT BACK.

Harvey MacKay

KEY EXPERIENCES

Your values are changing in a big way throughout 2014, and your relationships will come under the microscope as a result. You're serious about improving your love life and won't tolerate any sort of disrespect, mostly because you realise that you are worth more than what you previously thought.

As in 2013, Mars and Uranus continue to lift your spirits and your physical drive. You are active, and possibly even a little hot-blooded, so be careful not to react impulsively to the behaviour of others, especially if you are in intimate relationships with them.

Jupiter transits your career sector for a large part of the year, and up until August there will be considerable focus on improving your professional standing and skill set. Don't overdo things, as this planet has a tendency to push you beyond your limits. Take measured steps, especially if you are looking to do something new.

With Saturn in your zone of money, you'll be more judicious about the way you spend, and even if you don't earn more than you did last year, you'll still be able to set yourself up for a stable future.

ROMANCE AND FRIENDSHIP

You could feel somewhat unsettled as Uranus makes its way through your zone of marriage in 2014. This is not necessarily a bad thing, depending on how responsive your partner is to making changes and progressing your relationship. But it may not be as easy as you think.

Fortunately, Venus enters your zone of love affairs in late March and this could bring you a much better state of affairs. You will feel more relaxed about love, and if you're single, you'll have the opportunity to connect with those who are a good match for you.

With Mars in your Sun sign throughout the first part of the year, you are dynamic and, might I say, aggressive in going after what you feel you deserve. Ordinarily more balanced, you are likely to take a proactive approach to make sure that you are satisfied in all areas of your romantic and social life.

In the past, you may have been quite happy to play the peacemaker, but in the next twelve months, you will stand your ground on important ethical and life issues. This can extend to your social life, and your friends might be surprised to see your attitude change. As I said in the introduction, you are looking for more respect this year and, by posturing a little, you will get it.

Your social affairs and home life will feature strongly this year, and it is important to make sure that this aspect of your life is well looked after. If you have misgivings or are feeling pressured by loved ones and relatives, it will be difficult for you to enjoy your intimate relationships, particularly if you feel you're being judged by those who have no right to make those sort of assessments. Again, speaking your mind and letting others know exactly what you want is essential.

You may have had some practice in dealing with the unexpected throughout 2013, but be prepared for more of the same. In marriage, your spouse may be undergoing some unanticipated changes in work or health or may want a new lifestyle. If this is the case, adjustment will be one of your key words in 2014.

Relationships on the Rise

An impulsive attitude towards love and sex takes place when Venus and Mars enter a square aspect on the 17th of January. With the Sun also transiting your zone of love affairs on the 20th, this period will no doubt be a spicy one, so choose your partners wisely—and while you are sober! Regrets may be the aftermath of unbridled love and passion.

Interference by relatives during the first week of February will be unwelcome. You may feel that you need a justification for your actions, but this is not the case. Draw a line in the sand if people are meddling in your affairs.

SPOTLIGHT ON LOVE

More satisfaction in love can be expected when Venus enters your zone of love affairs on the 6th of March, and then between the 22nd and the 30th, when the Sun and Mars enter the same zone. You will have a more balanced approach to love and feel that your affections are being reciprocated.

Problems can occur in April with strong oppositional aspects from the Sun and Uranus. You are likely to overreact to the smallest provocation, and harmless statements may be taken personally. Additional exercise is not a bad idea throughout this month.

You can reach a new level of understanding in June when Venus transits the ninth zone of ethics, higher education and spiritual insight. Your relationship insights need to be practically implemented. This can happen after the 23rd, and it may even involve some sort of journey or connection to others in a distant place.

When the Sun transits the eleventh zone of friendship, you are likely to extend your circle of friends and acquaintances, which should be an enjoyable period, but around the 31st you may have problems with work and play overlapping. You need to be clear on boundaries, and those making a play for your affections should do the same.

Making important changes in your marriage can take place when Uranus is stationary in its motion, which happens on the 22nd of July. Up until October, you need to step up to the plate and not be afraid to implement the changes you feel are necessary to move your relationship forward. To some of you, this may be unsettling, but it's necessary to get your relationship back on track. Don't settle for anything less than what is going to make you happy in the long term.

Sidestep disputes between the 13th and the 17th of November as Mars, Uranus and the Sun challenge you. Excessive tiredness, distraction and overwork may impinge on your relationships, so try to control your moods and responses, particularly with those who are being confrontational. By maintaining your equanimity you also maintain control, and this is a key factor when it comes to enjoying better relationships throughout 2014.

WORK AND MONEY

Harness Your Moneymaking Powers

Making money can be summed up in an equation:

$$m\ (\$\ \text{money}) = e\ (\text{energy}) \times t\ (\text{time}) \times l\ (\text{love})$$

If one of these factors is not present—for example, energy or love—you could still make money, but you won't be ideally fulfilled in the process.

It's important to grasp the universal laws of attraction and success when dealing with money. It is also necessary to understand that when you love what you do, you infuse your work with the quality of attention, love and perfection. With these qualities you endow your work with a sort of electromagnetic appeal, a power that draws people to your work and makes them appreciate what you do. This generates a desire for people to use your service, buy your products and respect you for the great work you do. This will elevate you to higher and higher positions because you will be regarded as someone who exercises great diligence and skill in your actions.

Economy is your key word during 2014 as Saturn meanders through your zone of income and powerfully aspects your zone of shared finances. If you've been a spendthrift or you've had little regard for money and future security, this will change. Saturn is well known as the planet of thrift, economy and security. It is also the governing planet of concentration, focus and ambition. This means that you will be more serious about these issues and cut back on superfluous expenses, a strategy that will lead to a better financial position, even if you don't necessarily increase your income.

Neptune, one of the slow-moving planets, issues you a warning to be clear on borrowing and loaning. It may be difficult to refuse a loan when others put the hard word on you, but you have to be strong and realise that this is a sure-fire way of ruining a relationship. If you're in business, be careful not to go overboard if you are trying to expand your enterprise. This is shown by over-expansive Jupiter in your zone of professional activities.

One of the secrets to making more money throughout 2014 is the opposing aspect of Mars and Uranus. Mars, one of your key finance planets, is being challenged by the progressive planet Uranus. During these changing economic times, you need to be a step ahead of your competitors. This means looking for new ways to be creative and professional in the way you work.

It is not until the end of July or August that you are able to implement these new ideas as Mars is a little lazy in moving out of your Sun sign. At this point in time, you will feel a surge of energy to earn more money and make something more of your life.

Physical health is also important this year, so look at this area as a means of improving your earning capacity. A tired body is incapable of working to its optimum level. Try to balance your workload rather than doing too much. Pace yourself and, by all means, make sure you have a schedule that you can stick to. Although others may try to steer you off course with social and familial distractions, you need to exercise willpower to achieve your best this year.

Tips for Financial Success

Gaining insight into moneymaking opportunities can help you time your financial strategies, business meetings and other techniques for climbing the ladder of success.

Take on a leadership role, Libra, and be powerful and decisive in the way you execute your business decisions this year, especially from the 8th of January when Mars and the Sun combine in your Sun sign. Others will take note and give you the respect that is essential when doing business.

On the 2nd of March, Mars intensifies its energy, and you can do the same by intensifying your attitude and methods when conducting business with the general public or business partners.

If you're looking to acquire other people's money as seed capital for a business project, you can do so when the Sun enters the eighth zone of shared resources. Venture capitalists will be more than willing to listen to your business plan after the 20th of April, and it wouldn't hurt to learn the subtle art of manipulation to help accelerate your plans from the 4th of May.

One of the best tips I can give you this year is to work on your communication. This will be an excellent tool to focus on, particularly when Mars enters your finance sector on the 26th of July. Those of you in sales will be in a perfect position to sell your product or service, but be careful not to steamroll customers or would-be partners as Mars has a habit of being too aggressive.

Make a Donation

When the Sun enters the twelfth zone of humanitarianism and charity on the 23rd of August, making a small donation will actually lift your potential for earnings. Both philosophy and business believe in the value of charitable work and donations. The law of karma suggests that giving away a little increases your ability to earn more. Try this is an experiment.

Mars enters your fifth zone of speculation on the 5th of December, which means that you have the opportunity to invest money wisely and see a positive return for your efforts. Be prudent and you'll see some excellent financial returns.

Career Moves and Promotions

This is an important year for career moves due to the powerful influence of the planet Jupiter on your zone of profession for a large portion of the year.

You feel creative after the 20th of January as the Sun moves through your zone of creativity, investments and showmanship. If you are looking to make a move, this is the time to put your best foot forward and be noticed! You can also continue with this successful aura up until the 4th of February when the Sun makes excellent aspects to your Sun sign of Libra.

On the 19th and the 24th of February, strong ideals dominate your actions, but be careful as you may be overworked and tired. Hold off going for that job interview or asking for a pay rise as you may not be in the right frame of mind to be successful.

It's important to make a great impression on others, and on the 21st of March, when the sun moves into your zone of public relations, it is a wonderful time to showcase your talents to others. Try not to exaggerate them, however, because by the 1st of April you may appear too cocky, and this won't go down too well with those you are trying to impress for a job opportunity.

You can consolidate your talents and skills when Jupiter and Saturn enter into a wonderful trine aspect on the 25th of May. Talk to your employer and, based upon your steady work in the past, you may make some headway in acquiring that sought-after position.

Financial opportunities and an increase in income can occur between the 23rd and the 25th of July, and once again when the Sun enters the zone of finance on the 23rd of October. These transits indicate an increase in income, additional bonuses or commissions.

Hard work and a sustained effort from the 18th of November to the 15th of December spotlight the fact that you are able to acquire a good position and get a successful result in job interviews. Contracts may be a little difficult after the 24th, but this makes sense during the Christmas period. Tie up any loose ends before Christmas to benefit your career move.

When to Avoid Office Politics

There are some critical dates you should be mindful of when dealing with co-workers and employers in your place of work. This is because office politics, backstabbing and other untoward events are likely during this time.

Try to downplay your talents around the 12th of January when Jupiter and the Sun enter into a difficult aspect. Even if you try to share your successes with others, they may mistake you for a bragger and use this as an opportunity to shoot you down.

This same aspect occurs around the 29th of April, so even if you don't suspect anything is wrong, you may find that enemies, both secret and open, may come out of the woodwork around this time. On the same date, an eclipse occurs, indicating financial struggles or problems with those you have loaned money from or to. It's a good idea to get everything in writing this year to avoid any disputes over money.

Unfortunately, when Jupiter enters your zone of friendship on the 16th of July, you may be disappointed to find that someone you trusted has turned their back on you or undermined you in some way. Don't jump down their throat too quickly as this may be an inadvertent slip on their part. Investigate before you move into attack mode.

There could be confusion with co-workers on the 16th of November. Office politics may be confusing and you may not know how to deal with what's going on in the workplace. Silence is golden, as they say, and this is the best approach to take until the end of the year. Keep your cards close to your chest.

HEALTH, BEAUTY AND LIFESTYLE

Venus Calendar for Beauty

Venus, the planet of love, beauty and aesthetics, is your ruling planet, so its transit through the heavens is doubly important for those born under the sign of Libra. Powerful, direct movement of this planet on the 1st of February indicates an important turn-around in your self-awareness and self-image at this time. Up to and including the 6th of March, you will be feeling a lot more attractive and confident. From the 6th to the 22nd of March, you will be extremely attractive and others will be more likely to pay attention to you. As a result, this could be a very lucky period for your relationships, particularly romantic ones.

Marriage and other long-term commitments are affected by the way we look, and we all have to agree that physical attraction is the first point of contact with those we intend to spend the rest of our lives with. On the 3rd of May, Venus enters your seventh house of marriage and public relations. You won't have to do too much to impress others, and your charming aura will speak for itself.

Your attitude towards romance, love and beauty will continue to change, and after the 23rd of June, Venus will move to the outer part of your horoscope, indicating a deeper understanding of what constitutes beauty. Age, cultural circumstances and fads will recede into the background as you realise that inner happiness and peace are what make a person 'glow'. By gaining an understanding of this, you will soon see that your beauty is on the up and up.

> ## Beauty Tips
>
> You will get some useful beauty tips from friends after the 12th of August, and you'll be able to implement them by the 24th. This could be an opportunity to make dietary changes and try alternative techniques for improving the tone and lustre of your skin.

According to Hindu astrology, the second zone of the horoscope relates to the face. After the 24th of October, when Venus enters this sector, you will start to experience an increased radiance in your look. This may have something to do with the tips you have taken from friends. Overall, this should be an excellent year for beauty and increasing your self-esteem.

Showing off Your Libran Traits

This year you will learn that communication doesn't have to include words, it can also be non-verbal, and you will learn to use and implement this in many of your relationships.

Mercury and Venus are powerful on the 8th of January, and Mercury provides you with some very positive communication tools by the 8th of April. You will understand the intent of others more quickly due to your increased ability to listen.

Earlier, I mentioned the powerful transit of Venus on the 3rd of May to your zone of public relations. At the same time, Mercury makes some wonderful aspects on the 8th, 16th, 28th and 29th of May. This provides you with an upliftment in communications, networking skills and your ability to use social connections to improve your life.

You can really show off your star sign traits from the 19th of July due to the upwardly mobile Venus moving through the apex of your horoscope. This will give you a sense of accomplishment and wellbeing. Generally, every aspect of your life should fare quite well due to this transit, and it should continue into August when Venus moves into your zone of social connections on the 24th.

Venus is your ruling planet, and when a ruling planet enters your star sign—which in your case happens on the 30th of September—it marks the beginning of a very important cycle where many of your dreams can be fulfilled. You will also have powerful, seductive qualities that can be used (or abused) to achieve personal, sexual or business favours. Be careful not to overstep the mark.

November is a wonderful period for communication, contracts and binding agreements. Due to the strength of your Sun sign traits this year, you will be able to make excellent inroads in all of these areas and come out on top by the end of the year.

Best Ways to Celebrate

One of the key ingredients to happiness, joy and celebration this year is to keep Mars and Jupiter at bay. Both of these planets threaten to entangle you in disputes and past grievances. This may not seem to have much of a connection with the concept of celebration, but hanging onto grudges can rob you of moment-by-moment joy and celebration.

You need to be progressive this year, which means stepping away from disputes or people who provoke you. Remain happy, and with

Mercury, the Sun, Pluto and Venus commencing the year in your zone of inner happiness, it's imperative for you to take responsibility for how you react to circumstances. If you can do this, the period of the 6th of March should bring you many blessings, and part of your celebration should be rediscovering the creative joy in your personality.

You can take some of this creativity into your workplace between the 6th and the 18th of April and produce something unique that will be worth celebrating. This is not necessarily the celebration of a party, family get-together or workplace shindig. This has more to do with the joy of creating something out of personal focus, loving attention and spontaneous living.

Having said that, there are moments of exuberance that can be celebrated, and these relate to work and achievements that come from doing a job well, particularly after the 16th of July when Jupiter and Venus combine their energies to bring you some wonderful work opportunities. You could achieve something that you have been working toward for a long time, and this is worth celebrating.

On the 12th and 18th of August, the 12th and 14th of October, and the 18th of November, Venus gives you cause for celebration, and much of this has to do with being surrounded by loyal friends and supporters. There is nothing better than having the support of friends to make you feel that life is worth living and celebrating.

KARMA, SPIRITUALITY AND EMOTIONAL BALANCE

Much of your karmic energy this year is tied up with work and money. This is because Saturn, one of the planets of your future karma, is located in the finance sector. Your past karma is indicated by Mercury, so when these two planets enter into a favourable aspect, you can expect good fortune. Periods of excellent karma also occur around the 3rd of April when Mercury and Saturn move into their trine aspect.

Around the 8th and the 15th of April, Mercury moves into the vicinity of Uranus, another of your future karma planets. Expect sudden but pleasant tidings, good news or fateful opportunities through chance meetings. I say 'chance,' but we both know that there is no such thing and that these meetings come through the good deeds you have performed in this life and the previous one.

Earlier, I mentioned the importance of finding peace of mind through meditation, quiet time and rest. You will find an immense source of power from these practices as shown by the conjunction of Mercury and Pluto as 2014 commences. Mercury enters the fourth zone of peace and family contentment on the 17th of December. By focusing on your inner life and relationships you have overlooked in the past, you can find a great deal of solace and understanding in the latter part of the year.

A very significant transit also takes place when Saturn moves to your third zone of communication on the 24th of December. You will find yourself entering a new cycle, when communication can have an important impact on the people around you and, because the third house also has to do with siblings and neighbours, these people *may play a more prominent role in your life from now on.* You may even become their advisor or helper, but with Neptune in your sixth zone, this may not always work to your advantage. If you're playing the saviour, make sure you don't become a victim.

2014
MONTHLY & DAILY PREDICTIONS

IF YOU HAVE INTEGRITY, NOTHING ELSE MATTERS. IF YOU DON'T HAVE INTEGRITY, NOTHING ELSE MATTERS.

Alan Simpson

JANUARY

Monthly Overview

The start of the year will be busy and your schedule could become untenable. Demands on the home front create friction, especially on the 1st, 4th, 7th, 9th and 17th. Try not to accommodate too many people as you will not get anything done. Jupiter's influence on your career sector means that opportunities can develop, but you need to balance work and play.

1. You are unlikely to accept affection or even an apology today, but forgiveness is your key word for the rest of the year. Try to be less harsh with loved ones at home.

2. Productivity will come as a result of deeper analysis of a situation or problem. As a result, you can move on to something new and more lucrative.

3. You need to explore new environments if you are looking for love, and right now the combined influence of Venus and Mars is positive. Enjoy making new acquaintances.

4   You must exude power today if you want to gain the respect that you desire. Important or influential people may cross your path today.

5   If you are confused about the direction you should choose, a close friend may lend support and help you re-orient yourself.

6   You need to make contact with people who have a different angle on health and dietary issues. Expand your understanding to improve your wellbeing.

7   You need a diversion today, something that will distract you from your normal routine, especially in your relationship. Business trips also fare well.

8   You can overcome set backs on the home front through appropriate communication with those who have been causing problems. You will be received well for the effort you make.

9   If financial matters have been moving slowly, you will find that the pace steps up today. Discuss banking issues, if necessary.

10   Your strong emotions are the key to resurrecting a relationship that you thought was on the rocks. Keep up the intensity, even if it's uncomfortable for the other person.

11 You mustn't give up if an obstacle presents itself. If you have been trying to make peace with someone, they will be reluctant to reciprocate. Tenacity is your key word now.

12 You have overlooked a romantic or social opportunity, but it will now come to light and reward you with some pleasure.

13 Disputes come to a head and a judgment is made. The news you hear should be favourable.

14 Sleepless nights may be bothering you, but worrying about professional matters should be left to a more appropriate time.

15 You will be mentally and physically recharged, and whatever problems you had may suddenly disappear. A health concern may turn out to be nothing.

16 Finances are the focus now, and although you are self-sufficient, you are fearful about the future. This is of no use to you, so continue to do what you do best.

17 Your relationships can help you forge new contacts that increase your wealth and professional acumen. A new business alliance can be formed at this time.

18 New ideas may come to light, but these are best appreciated alone. Time out is necessary to do your best work today.

19 Cutting corners to make quick money is inadvisable now. Make sure you have a business plan in place before you rush madly into the unknown.

20 You may have thought that something was lost or that you were out of the running, but news will turn things around and give you cause for optimism.

21 You could be overemotional and moody today. Once you make a decision, stick to it.

22 A disappointment may be a blessing in disguise. What appears to be a misfortune will turn out to be advantageous in the future.

23 If you've been reluctant to voice your displeasure to someone, you will now be able to communicate how you feel—much to their surprise. You can now move forward without obstruction.

24 You know that you need to earn more money, but your workload may be daunting just now. You have to complete old tasks before you embark on new ones.

25 You may inherit a position or situation that is bigger than you anticipated. Do some research before accepting the new role.

26 Doing some charitable work will help balance your karma. Besides, you will feel good doing someone a favour today.

27 Don't share too much information with others as there are elements of deception and treachery in the air. Hold your cards close to your chest.

28 You need to exert your influence on family members who are not pulling their weight, but be fair as you don't want to alienate anyone in the process.

29 You have the power to express yourself creatively now. This will give you a greater sense of self-worth and bolster your physical and emotional wellbeing.

30 There could be some frustration surrounding children or those less mature than you. Patience is your key word today.

31 You may have to surrender some of your time to help those who are less capable than you. This could cost you money, but you will gain some benefits in the future.

FEBRUARY

Monthly Overview

This is a more relaxed month, with entertainment and social or love affairs being more prominent. A new relationship is likely to commence this month, or you will have the opportunity to reignite an old flame. Mercury's entry into your zone of work on the 13th indicates some hustle and bustle in the workplace and the implementation of new methods for improving your professional activities. This is also accentuated on the 19th when the Sun also adds its energy to the mix. Some unexpected changes in your work and relationships require you to think quickly on the 26th.

---

1 The focus now is on friends, but you may vacillate in your opinion of someone. Being decisive may require a little more time.

---

2 You are lucky at the moment and can achieve what you want through careful analysis, communication and even the manipulation of circumstances. You may also want to indulge yourself at a spa or beauty parlour today.

3 Things seem stationary right now. The secret is not to push things; just let them happen. Later in the day, spend a little quiet time reflecting.

4 There may be tension with others because you are not speaking your mind about something they have done to you. This will be upsetting unless you lay your cards on the table.

5 Cut back on excessive habits such as drinking, smoking or overeating. This may cause you problems and interfere with your work.

6 It's time to renegotiate your contract, and you can do so from a position of strength. Your determination is renewed today.

7 Take care as the information you require is not forthcoming. Making decisions without the appropriate facts may catch you out later.

8 A promising financial plan may stall right now. Look for an alternative.

9 You may want to take it easy, but someone is demanding that you do otherwise. If you don't have the energy to help someone today, postpone it until a more appropriate time.

10 Disputes about money are likely now. This is because you haven't been clear on what you think is fair or unfair. Don't allow yourself to feel obligated.

11 Your emotions are adversely effected by Uranus today, so you need to move slowly and think more clearly before reacting to others. A lover may not act in the way that you wish them to.

12 You are trying to control your feelings today, but others may be provoking you. You need to put the 'do not disturb' sign up on the door.

13 It's best to entertain at home today as you won't have the energy to rush from destination to destination. Dinner with intimate friends will be pleasurable.

14 Better the devil you know than the devil you don't. You may wish to swap one relationship for another, but you'll realise at the last minute that you've made the wrong decision.

15 You may be feeling emotionally down, and the worst thing you can do is get lazy. Get up and do some sport or exercise; this will refresh you.

16 You may be doing quite well at work, but some doubts may arise today. If you dwell on this too much, your world could come crashing down on you. Remain positive.

17 You are able to shoulder new responsibilities now and embark on a new moneymaking venture. If you are an entrepreneur, this is the start of something new and positive.

18 Friends or family members may be taking advantage of you financially. If you have loaned money and it has not been returned, it would be foolish to do it again.

19 You could be excessive today because many of the aspects are difficult right now. You have a lot on your plate and could be trying to please too many people.

20 You will receive a message or email that gives you the green light to proceed along a desired path. Unfortunately, you may be creatively blocked. Remember, you don't have to do everything right now.

21 There is no need to feel anxious, particularly if you are surrounded by well-wishers and fun people. You may be feeling inadequate and lacking some self-assurance. Go with the flow and have fun today.

22 You may have strong feelings for someone who you feel is culturally inappropriate. Maintain your friendship, but don't cross the line.

23 You are experiencing feelings of upliftment and creative power just now, so it's the perfect time to explore what's on offer. Develop a hobby or investigate how you can express yourself more adequately.

24 Before you can create something in this world, you need to envision or creatively imagine what it is. Meditation or other relaxation practices will help you tap into these inner resources.

25 Difficult legal matters or bureaucratic issues will bother you right now. You may need the help of a professional to solve them.

26 Someone you trusted may betray you, and this could shatter your world. Don't let this impinge on new relationships that are forming.

27 You have the ability to teach or instruct others on the proper course of action to be taken. You may discover a talent that you didn't realise you had.

28 You want to take things more slowly, even though you are impulsive today. You could be annoyed by changing schedules and the fact that someone else is calling the shots.

MARCH

Monthly Overview

Mercury moves into its forward motion, allowing you to complete tasks that you were unable to complete earlier. Your mind and thinking are much clearer. Health matters need to be watched as Mars' activity is unpredictable, especially after the 2nd. An excellent cycle commences after the 6th when Venus enters your zone of love and romance. Your creative energies will be considerable at this time. Try not to make a hasty decision on the 11th. On the 19th, an unexpected surprise will lift your spirits, and on the 21st, when the sun enters the zone of marriage, you will feel elation over your relationships.

---

1 You may not have the support of others today, but you do have the backing of someone who will be instrumental in helping you complete your tasks. You can thank Mercury for that.

---

2 You are searching for meaning, but this is not something you can extract from others. You need to contemplate the deeper mysteries of life and allow your inner self to reveal the answers.

---

3 Your feelings are oscillating right now and you can't figure out whether you should continue with a relationship or pull back. There is no harm in exploring the relationship and making your decision later.

4 Adverse conditions could come as a bit of a surprise today. You need to plan your work more effectively and have an alternative strategy on hand.

5 You could be apprehensive about expressing your feelings towards someone, especially if they have hurt you in the past. On the other hand, your work is flourishing right now and you may prefer to put your energy into this area.

6 Being separated from your peer group or the one you love is not a bad thing. It will give you the opportunity to gain some perspective.

7 You could feel upset by the news you receive just now, but you'll be more disturbed by the fact that a decision may depend on this information. That decision may not be easy.

8 You are confused about your relationships today, particularly those in which your values differ greatly from the other person's. Don't compromise for the sake of winning their approval.

9 Don't allow yourself to be irritated by a work associate. It's up to you to maintain a cool response under pressure.

10 You need to get out and about today, so a shopping spree might be in order. Be careful, though, as spontaneity may get you into trouble, particularly if you spend too much.

11 Others are trying to control you, but you are not going to be putting up with it. Your power will catch people off guard today.

12 Although you are deriving a lot of satisfaction from work, you could be doing too much too soon. Pace yourself or you may run yourself into the ground.

13 Conflicts are likely now, but you may not know how to deal with them. You will feel restricted or unable to take control due to extenuating circumstances.

14 You may have to make a judgment against someone. This will be uncomfortable because it may be interpreted as favouritism. Stick to the truth, as this is the only course of action you can take.

15 You may miss an opportunity because you have taken your eye off the ball. Make arrangements to receive information in your absence. This is also a day when speculation may pay off.

16   Someone may reveal a secret to you, and this could cause you anxiety. Carrying confidential matters in your heart may bother you.

17   If you are dealing with someone opinionated today, you will have a hard time biting your tongue. Look deeper into the underlying causes of this behaviour. The person may be insecure.

18   You may be overcompensating for the fact that you are not feeling loved today. Trying to get this affection from others could make you appear needy. Be careful.

19   Unless you take the phone off the hook, you may be inundated by calls today. This will erode your time, making it difficult for you to finish your work.

20   There are positive changes afoot in your relationships and financial affairs. These areas may overlap today and bring you good fortune. Try not to be too obsessive as this could cause disruptions in your personal relationships.

21   You may get bogged down by faulty appliances, electrical problems or computing issues. At the end of the day, you will learn something from this experience.

22   There will be disputes over money today. If you are in a business partnership, it may be necessary to clearly redefine your roles in the venture.

23   It may be a time of endings for some relationships, but this is essential for growth and for new relationships to commence.

24   If you are unable to solidify an idea and make it practical, share it with someone who can help you. Don't be selfish with your creative output today.

25   Plans may be cancelled today, and someone may blame you. Quietly explain the situation to help them understand.

26   Expect some recognition for your work, but don't let this go to your head. Keep improving your professional excellence.

27   You may learn financial lessons from a casual discussion with a successful woman. Someone in a healing profession will open your eyes to new alternatives.

28   You will have a burst of energy today and get a lot done. Don't waste the opportunity.

29   It's a time of healing now, and some of your emotional wounds will resurface so you can re-examine them. Don't be scared to confront them.

30 Don't allow past emotional hurts to obstruct you from experiencing true love. Superimposing the past on the present is a mistake.

31 Temperance is your key word today, but it may be difficult in your current circumstances. Use your willpower.

APRIL

Monthly Overview

Don't expect too much of yourself this month as you may not be able to deliver. Make sure you have the requisite strength, knowledge and skills to attempt a task that is a little out of your depth. You have excellent negotiation skills on the 8th, but you may need to change elements of the agreement due to an oversight. You will need to sidestep those who are out to blackmail you on the 21st.

---

1 You may come across as insensitive, especially if you forget a promise that you made to someone. Try to remember your commitments before going into meetings.

---

2 You may seem too serious to others today, so allow your sense of humour to dictate your behaviour today.

---

3 You may have some fears about something happening in a relationship, but these are unfounded. You are projecting your own ideas onto a situation. Try to see things as they really are.

4 Messages could be a little fuzzy today, so don't be afraid to clarify what is said. The repercussions could be confusing and time-consuming.

5 You may take an interest in metaphysical, psychic or spiritual topics, so it's a good time to delve into these things and establish a strong foundation of understanding.

6 Someone may be forcing ideas down your throat. Listen to them, even though you may be irritated by their style.

7 If you decide to travel, even if it's a short journey, expect some good fortune and chance meetings that will bring a smile to your face.

8 You will want to postpone some of your work just now, probably because it's too tedious and you're feeling a little lazy. If you have a rest, it will give you the energy to come back with full force.

9 You are making big plans, but don't overstep the mark. Try to schedule your activities and have a long-term agenda that you can stick to. This will ensure success.

10 Negative circumstances in your relationship will end because you can see situations that are worse than yours. This makes you realise how lucky you are.

11 Helping friends or relatives with a problem may deplete your energy today. Protect yourself if you are going to play the role of the saviour.

12 You may have put someone on a pedestal, only to find that your perception was way off. Remember, everyone is human and has faults—including you.

13 You're not feeling well today because you are overthinking a situation that is affecting you physically. Do your best and leave the rest to providence.

14 You will be concerned about expenses and the fact that you drew some rash conclusions. You may find the same product or service at a cheaper price, but it's too late now.

15 You are tense and possibly even angry. This is a transit when errors of judgment and injuries may occur. Take your time and rethink your position.

16 You may want to impress someone with a new meal, but you could ruin the whole thing through inexperience and poor preparation. Stick with the tried and tested today.

17 You need to reclaim your territory, especially if someone has assumed that your space and possessions are theirs. This may not be an easy task.

18 You have been too passive when it comes to handling your finances, so it's time to step up and make amends. You will be surprised at how much ground you can cover once you make the decision.

19 You may feel embarrassed when someone puts the hard word on you for a loan, be it financial or material. You need to clarify your position and explain that you don't want to jeopardise the friendship.

20 You have to amend your philosophical beliefs because they are not helping you solve your problems. This is the start of a new phase of spiritual growth for you.

21 If you didn't graduate from college, it doesn't mean that you can't learn new tricks. Your potential to learn is strong. Make the effort to increase your intellectual abilities.

22 You are emotional at the moment, which is making it difficult for you to use reason within your relationships. Don't allow your emotions to cloud your common sense.

23 You are a big thinker today, and others may not be able to keep up with you. Try to break down your ideas into smaller components for those less ambitious than you.

24 The number eight is lucky for you right now, but luck is also a state of mind, and if you feel bitter about a situation, that energy could be polluting your circumstances. Take each moment as it comes and don't rely on the past to make your decisions.

25 You feel better today and the planets are providing supportive aspects. You feel that life is a journey of discovery at present, but make sure you surround yourself with friends who are like-minded.

26 You need to open up your mind to modern music styles. Drop your preconceptions and enjoy the moment. You may be invited to a party that's a little different from what you're accustomed to.

27 Your greatest successes will come from working behind the scenes and communicating your ideas through written or electronic forms.

28 You could be taken aback by someone's seductive overtures. You may not be seeing yourself the way others do.

29 You have had enough of drama and will opt to remain silent when you hear gossip and innuendo. This is the best position you can take.

30 Confronting someone is the best tactic, even if they retaliate. You will come out a winner and get more respect from them.

☀ MAY ☀

👤 Monthly Overview

This is a great month for your self-esteem and for improving your relationships, both personal and professional. On the 3rd, when Venus moves to your zone of marriage, you could be part of a celebration, such as a christening, engagement or wedding. This may also relate to your relationship and increased feelings of love and warmth. When Mercury transits your zone of career on the 29th, expect more calls, emails and other communication.

---

1 A dreary farewell has put a damper on your day. You'll simply have to grin and bear it.

---

2 You're on the defensive today, but with a little clever manoeuvring you'll come out the winner. Don't allow others to use their seniority to demean you.

---

3 Someone you love may not be well, and you'll need to assist them in their time of need. This will be greatly appreciated.

4 You want to straighten out some key areas in your life and should have no trouble doing this. As long as you can overcome your lazy urge, all will be well.

5 Sometimes a situation is not fair, and you will be irritated by the fact that you are not able to bring justice to the table. The best you can do is conduct yourself in a way that sets a good example.

6 If you're single, you may be wondering about an associate and whether or not a relationship can ensue. Try not to mix business with pleasure as this can complicate the situation.

7 Domestic affairs are exciting, but they can come with some additional responsibilities. You feel as if you have an unbelievable amount of work to clear off the table, but don't forget that there are other members of the family who can help.

8 You're presented with some eye-opening news that can help you financially. There may be some cost involved with this. Investigate the matter further.

9 Do you qualify as hip? You may feel that you don't quite fit in with a new group of friends. Simply be yourself.

10 You have a chance to enjoy some pleasure now, but you need to set aside the time to do it. Finding excuses will only result in circumventing those opportunities again and again.

11 You have to look at the root causes of ill health, and these may not be what you think. Simply relying on a doctor to solve them is a cop-out. Study your lifestyle and diet.

12 You're probably thinking of the past now, and this is making you feel nostalgic. You need to cut your ties with memories that make you feel bad.

13 You have some problems in your knee or hip, so pay attention to your posture, stance, the shoes you wear and the type of furniture you are using.

14 Wear something a little different as an experiment. Believe it or not, it will change your self-image dramatically.

15 It's time to have a heart to heart with your significant other and clear the air. This may bring up topics that are uncomfortable, but in the end it will improve matters.

16 Cash flow and business profits could be slow just now. You have to be clever in the way you manage your financial affairs.

17 You want to travel during this cycle as the Moon moves through your ninth zone of long journeys, but are your finances up to it? At the very least you can start to plan.

18 With the influence of Pluto you can transform a simple situation into something magical. You need to dig deep and be creative. A sibling may be instrumental in helping you do this.

19 You still have a desire for travel, and you may discuss travel plans with someone over the phone. Take your time.

20 Some postponed actions will resurface, and you'll be in a better position to gain the upper hand. Your intuition is correct, so trust it.

21 You could be worried about the financial and professional circumstances of your partner or spouse. Support doesn't have to be verbal. Being there for them will be enough.

22 Protect your creative ideas, as others are likely to copy or even steal your intellectual property. Be selective about who you share this information with.

23 You can make a resolution and stick to it now, particularly if you want to overcome a habit. This means changing your circle of friends and sticking to your resolve.

24 If you're feeling out of sorts, it could be because you're comparing yourself to others. Accept yourself for who you are, and capitalise on that.

25 You want to pursue spiritual interests but your ideas may not be accepted by others. Keep these matters to yourself.

26 You are more apt to share your feelings with someone who is going through similar life experiences. This will help you cope.

27 Some of you may decide to resume tertiary studies or go to an evening college to further your knowledge. This will develop your skill set and open new doorways to social interaction.

28 You'll be able to balance your expenses with your income during this short phase of positive influence between Mercury and Venus. Put a little aside for a rainy day.

29 You could be afraid of fixing something around the home because of the cost. Just remind yourself that you deserve the best, even if it does reduce your bank balance a little.

30   You may have to be the spokesperson for some cause or project at work. If you're not comfortable about this, speak up or you could find yourself overwhelmed with additional responsibilities.

31   You need to be insistent to get your way today. If an employer or manager has been slow to respond, this is the only way to get them to come around.

JUNE

Monthly Overview

Your love of art and culture increases this month, and around the 4th, when Venus and Neptune make contact, this will be evident. Take care after the 7th, however, when Mercury, the planet of communication and agreements, moves retrograde. You will need to investigate information more thoroughly before making a commitment. On the 18th, a generous dose of energy from Venus and Jupiter may fast-track your career moves. This is the perfect time to ask for a pay rise or new position. After the 21st, when the Sun enters your career zone and Venus enters your zone of luck on the 23rd, you will find good karma coming your way.

---

1 You may be overinflating your abilities in order to impress others. They will be disappointed when they find that you're not up to the task. Keep it real.

2 You want to see changes on the home front, but you have to take drastic measures to break free of oppressive circumstances. Now is not the time.

3   You could enjoy making purchases for your domestic environment, but make sure that the furniture matches the décor. A little more planning is necessary.

4   Others may disapprove of a decision that you or your partner have made, but this is none of their business. Don't be discouraged or disheartened by their opinions.

5   It's a busy day today, and you may have difficulty choosing one activity over another. Don't overwhelm yourself. Focus on one person at a time.

6   You have the power to uplift others through example, experience and kindness. Even if you don't see an immediate result, the seeds of change have been sown.

7   Your past karma will now yield good results due to the positive actions you have performed. Some good fortune should come to light.

8   If you avoid the paperwork for an important financial matter, you'll only be making a rod for your own back. Tedium may be part of the routine now, but it is essential.

9   You could be keen to commence a new enterprise on someone's advice, but you have not done enough research. Take care to dot your i's and cross your t's.

10 Someone could make you feel as if you don't understand them, but you've got the picture crystal clear. Don't be swayed into assuming you've made an error.

11 You can find innovative new ways to deal with professional opportunities by stepping outside the square. This will be an exciting time.

12 A friend may be forcing you to attend a function or do something against your will. Maintain your integrity today.

13 Conflicting signals and nonverbal communication from your partner or lover may bother you today. Play it cool as the wrong response could cause a flare up.

14 You could be worried about health issues today, but these could be largely psychosomatic. Don't pay much attention to the odd twitch or twinge.

15 You don't have telepathic powers today, so you should rely on rational thought. This will be advantageous in a business meeting.

16 Take the time to be better informed before making an important choice regarding your profession. Tension between you and others could cause you to make errors.

17 You need to blend elegance and originality to win the hearts of your colleagues or friends. This will help you stand out from the crowd.

18 Making a strong commitment to someone before getting to know them may cause regret. Ask the serious questions.

19 You want to take the helm but may find yourself ill-equipped to do so. Let someone else take control today.

20 Your instincts about health are quite strong today. If you know exactly what needs to be done, do it, even if you've been advised otherwise.

21 Don't judge others on face value today as their motivations may be different from what you suspect. You may even learn something from their style.

22 You're not in the mood for initiating intimate or sexual encounters of any sort today. You may prefer to read a book or zone out in front of the television.

23 Don't be afraid to ask for help. There may be someone you feel uncomfortable with, but they may have the information and support structure you require.

24 Your thoughts are far away today, and this may affect your performance. Try to ground yourself.

25 Your attitude to money could be somewhat emotional at the moment, which will make you believe anything that people tell you. This could cost you dearly.

26 Believing everything you hear is not advisable now. If you cut corners, you're likely to be seen as gullible and naïve. Don't be afraid to refute statements that are obviously false.

27 Today you may be fighting for your rights, but do you really know what you want? Be clear on this or you could find yourself in over your head when articulating the specifics of your grievances.

28 You may hit a brick wall with someone in a negotiation. This could be a simple agreement between you and a friend or close relative. Compromise is your key word today.

29 You may feel inspired today, but you need a close ally who can help make things happen. This is a day of imagination mixed with adventure.

30 You could be stressed today, and friends will only confuse you with their version of what you should do to rectify the situation. Think for yourself.

JULY

Monthly Overview

The 1st of the month gives you the green light to execute your plans, and up until the 9th you will be taking your responsibilities more seriously and making your dreams a reality. Finances between the 9th and the 13th should improve, as should your ability to speak up for what you believe you deserve. You can thank Mercury for this. More social activities associated with your work and colleagues are likely from the 16th up until the 23rd. You may be dreaming of love, but you need to understand the ramifications of your actions between the 24th and 28th. Don't be impulsive in your relationships.

1 You mustn't let emotional disturbances impact on your professional activities today. You need to remain objective, but this is not going to be achieved if you keep dwelling on personal matters.

2 You will be confused about a relationship right now. If you're single, the issue will be whether to remain friends or cross the line. Curiosity may get the better of you.

3 Your energy today is boundless, and you'll be able to achieve a great deal. Just make sure that your timetable can accommodate the additional work.

4 You need to make last minute calculations before you go on a spending spree today. Remember, even modest savings can add up to quite a bit over time.

5 Relationships with women run smoothly now, and you'll benefit from the advice of one or two. This can give you the emotional strength that's necessary now.

6 You're out of step with an authority figure today, but a sense of goodwill will calm the storm. Don't feel intimidated by their power.

7 You have clear objectives just now, and you'll make a great impression on the general public. Decisions are likely to be correct, and spontaneous action is favoured.

8 Your mind is inquisitive at the moment, and you'll be busy trying to ferret out information to improve yourself and your relationships. It's an excellent time to read self-help books.

9 You could feel destabilised as the current environment changes. Adjustment is your key word, and don't forget the concept of survival of the fittest.

10 You may have a topsy-turvy relationship, but that doesn't mean that you have to throw out the baby with the bath water. Listen to each other's side of the story.

11 You'd like to feel more constructive, but your thinking is muddled. It may be better to postpone an appointment or important meeting.

12 It's a problematic day today, and minor tensions will pile up and cause a change in plans. Try to keep your mind on an even keel.

13 You want to help someone, but they may not be amenable to your suggestions. Sometimes it's better to let people sort out their own issues.

14 You're pushy today, and too much friction will create fire. You may have difficulties of an idealistic nature and your views may not be in harmony with those around you.

15 You want to accumulate more friends during this cycle, but quality is better than quantity. Cut back rather than increase your social connections at present.

16 You may be a little obsessive about getting to the bottom of a problem, and this will irritate others. Try to coax them rather than holding a gun to their head.

17 You may run into conflicts today, and no amount of communication will solve them. It's a case of oil and water not mixing.

18 Several short trips are necessary now, but this may involve a dispute. The experience may be not altogether pleasant.

19 Allow the past to recede rather than holding on to it. Someone may remind you of some past incidents that could ruin your day. Don't allow this to happen.

20 You may need to take time out to rethink your professional position. If you have long service leave or sick pay owing, it's a good time to take it.

21 Although you crave affection and a deeper connection with your loved one, they may not be in a position to give it to you. They may be overworked and sorting through some problems.

22 There may be an oversight or missed appointment due to poor record-keeping on your part. Try to get your diary in order.

23 Keeping track of family members maybe a headache now. Co-ordinating your schedule with youngsters is also a challenge.

24 You need to increase trade through the use of marketing, advertising and social networking. You could be missing out on some of the benefits of new technology.

25 You could be superimposing a past romantic experience on your current one. Try to look at your relationship in a new light.

26 Plans to meet someone could be sidelined for something that has greater priority. This may cause a lack of enthusiasm in the other person. You may need to win them over again.

27 You may not be aware of it, but your family will be your best source of support at present. Try to acknowledge the help you're getting.

28 Try to be more financially assertive, especially when it comes to expenditures on the home front. You may need to budget for food and domestic supplies.

29 You could become a little disillusioned about a relationship, but being assertive and extracting an opinion over some matter will help get the friendship back on track.

30 Some of your investments will pay off now, but think carefully about what you want to do with that money. It may be idea good idea to reinvest it.

31 Something you've been waiting for may take longer to arrive. You'll receive what you desire, but patience will be necessary.

AUGUST

Monthly Overview

Sharing your thoughts and dreams with others will help solidify your ambitions, and up until the 9th you have the perfect opportunity to do this. You will be busy preparing for outings and engagements and may play a core role in the preparation or management of these events. You continue to attract friends throughout the month, and the 12th is significant as Venus moves to the eleventh zone of friendship and social activities. By the 23rd you will need some time out as the Sun moves to the quiet area of your horoscope. Watch your health around the 30th.

---

1   You can spot a hypocrite a mile away today, but it may be someone that you need to deal with on regular basis. As long as you know the truth, you won't be taken in.

2   You can create a more interesting work environment today by embracing different technologies and new methods of doing things. However, this may not be easy. Falling into old habits may be your biggest obstruction.

3 Trying to get something done without too much effort is going to work against your best interests. You may have other things on your mind, but don't sacrifice quality for the sake of expediency.

4 You could be cluttering your life with too many things and, more importantly, too many people who don't add any value. You need to clear your thinking and ignore the opinions of others.

5 Your partner may not be reciprocating the passion that you want just now. Rather than being lazy about this, be creative and find new ways of stimulating the relationship. The *Kama Sutra* may be of interest to you.

6 A change is as good as a holiday, and today you need to get out of your normal routine and mix things up. You could be feeling bogged down by the same people and the same environment.

7 The only way to achieve a position of valuable employment is to do adequate research and seek out people in the know. These positions aren't going to fall into your lap.

8 You have to initiate a project and prove yourself before others will give you the green light on more important projects. By taking the lead you will emerge the victor.

9 You could be feeling unmotivated and irritated. Get over this phase and focus on the things that are of importance.

10 You're immunity could be low, so look into what can cause lethargy, sickness and long-term disease. Stress is a factor that can contribute to a lowered immune system.

11 You have an interest in psychology and will be fascinated by people and what motivates them. You'll start to see your usual group of friends and relatives in a completely different light.

12 You're in the mood for a bit of fun, even skylarking. This is a great way to relieve your current stress.

13 You'll be asked to amend some of your work processes. Rather than bucking the system, go along with it as you may learn something new.

14 Be independent today and try not to talk and act the way others do. Developing a unique style will be your challenge throughout this coming period.

15 You need to master some hobby or creative activity that will give you an aim outside of your usual work and family demands. This will give you a new lease on life.

16   Be careful of criminals and those who are likely to be dishonest and deceptive. You have the opportunity to clear the decks of people who are untrustworthy.

17   Someone close to you has become an expert in isolating themselves, and it may be difficult for you to bring them out of themselves. Using force will only push them further away.

18   You may feel as if you've been short-changed in some way. Develop the art of gratitude, even if you feel hard done by.

19   Mercury and Neptune create a confusing state of affairs today. You need to communicate clearly and succinctly. This will avoid misunderstandings.

20   If you've been addicted to some sort of habit, it's time to reassert your resolutions and turn over a new leaf. You'll feel a great sense of power when you exert your will in this way.

21   You're being forced to do something you don't want to do and will dig in your heels against great opposition. Practice makes perfect, so don't close the door on this completely.

22   A rapid friendship could mean rapid deterioration. Move more slowly if you find that your carnal instincts are overtaking your sensibilities.

23   To be influential in the home and improve the behaviour of those younger than yourself, you need to take the initiative and set the perfect example. Children and their needs will feature strongly at this time.

24   You need to set up a barrier, a sort of restraint against people who are taking liberties with you. If people are treading all over you, you need to make changes.

25   You'll expand your mental horizons and discover new things about yourself and others, particularly in the realm of love. Your mind is clear on what you want and you should be able to articulate this.

26   Mars in Saturn creates a frustrating state of affairs in your relationship and business partnerships today. You're covering up your emotions, and there is a risk that you'll explode. It's better to speak now rather than cut off someone's head later.

27   There's a continuing need to get rid of things that are obsolete in your life, such as objects, methodologies and people. You're not feeling appreciated, which means eliminating things that inhibit this.

28 You're receiving mystical insights into how you should manage your work more efficiently—but you're ignoring them. Sit quietly and listen with your heart rather than your mind.

29 Your planned destination may be sidelined for something completely different. There's a sense of excitement surrounding the unknown.

30 Today is all about adapting to people and circumstances that you find yourself in. You need to make provisions for a situation that you are not quite ready for.

31 Correspondence of an unusual nature will take your fancy, and meeting people online will be the beginning of some new, long-term relationships.

SEPTEMBER

Monthly Overview

You want to restart some spiritual activities during this month, and when Venus moves to your twelfth zone of karma and meditative practices on the 6th, it's a good time to consider this. Don't allow confusion or vague ideas to interfere with your perception of the truth on the 10th. Mars enters the third zone of bustling activity on the 14th, but by the 22nd you may be worn out and confused about the outcome. Get clarification before throwing away good money. Your energy returns to normal around the 23rd with the solar return to Libra.

---

1 Someone's unacceptable behaviour may require you to intervene and take drastic steps for the good of the group. You mustn't feel embarrassed about eliminating this behaviour from your life.

---

2 It's vital that you store up energy now, very much like saving for a rainy day. Don't waste it on useless activities and people.

3 The mainstream is annoying you right now, and you may choose to buy a book or watch a movie that is completely different from your usual tastes. This will kick-start a new level of creativity within you.

4 It's okay to be a little silly if you're feeling romantic. Discovering the inner child is part and parcel of letting go.

5 If you're the boss in your workplace, you may have to sack someone now. Exerting power is necessary, and eliminating someone who's not pulling their weight is the fair thing to do for everyone concerned.

6 Age is a state of mind, and if you're inclined to worry about the years slipping by, it's best to forget time and get actively involved in something you love.

7 You're full of physical energy today, but your mind may not be a willing participant. If you're forced to do something against your will, you will respond negatively.

8 You won't be ashamed to terminate a friendship that has exceeded its use-by date. There are greener pastures to explore.

9 If you're feeling constraints in your life, you'll turn around and ask why. Those imposing limitations on you won't have an answer. The solution is to do your own thing.

10 You have to be smart with your wallet as Mercury and Pluto indicate obsessive tendencies to spend without thought. This is worse if someone is demanding that you spend on their behalf.

11 You have to take some risks now, and this relates to the spiritual dimension of your life. Don't be afraid to think differently and change your destiny.

12 You have a prime opportunity to change the way others see you. Creating a new aura will fascinate and impress others.

13 You are probably feeling annoyed that you've become a slave to electronic devices. This is a time to turn your phone off and simply enjoy the sun, sky and deep blue sea without the irritating buzz of someone intruding into your life.

14 You need to reinforce your security by checking locks, alarms and security cameras. Keep a tighter hold on your personal belongings when travelling in groups or crowds.

15 Who's the killjoy in the group? Someone may be putting a damper on your enjoyment. If this is the case, you need to short-circuit them and not have anything to do with them anymore.

16 You could get a glowing report for the work you've done, but try not to boast about it. There may be envious co-workers lurking in the shadows who are ready to tear you down.

17 You've underestimated your ability to add value by consulting and sharing your expertise. There could be additional income streams that may develop out of this talent.

18 You may not trust someone whose beliefs are masking devious behaviour. Trust your instincts.

19 If you're hiring people to do work for you, particularly construction, you may feel that some aspects of the work are unsafe. You can demand certain standards and check their insurance policies as well.

20 You need to look into organics, the environment and healthy living. A slight modification in your lifestyle will ensure a better quality of life.

21 You could be trying to checkmate another person only to find that all your efforts are worthless. Don't waste your valuable time on useless activities.

22 If you're seeking legal or financial advice from someone, you need to shape their opinions and advice. After all, you're the one paying them for the service.

23 You might find yourself planning an evening, only to be distracted by something that goes wrong. This is the proverbial vampire night!

24 Today's New Moon encourages you to uplift yourself and move into a higher gear. This is the beginning of a new work or lifestyle program that should be embraced.

25 There are ways and means of reducing your bills, and one of them is to change your method of paying off loans. Rather than making monthly payments, consider fortnightly or even weekly payments. The financial benefits will be immense.

26 You want to capture memories just now, so you'll be aggressive in using your camera or jotting down notes in your diary. There is a lot of activity going on, so don't lose these memories.

27 You're feeling socially overwhelmed and want a quality one-on-one relationship. You and your partner need to make the time for each other during this cycle.

28 You have to reflect back the kindness that you receive in your relationships. This sets up a bio-feedback where good feeds good, generosity increases profitability and love creates more love.

29 You're open to emotional expression just now. In fact, you want it badly. You're likely to create a more loving environment so that your partner can feel comfortable sharing his or her feelings with you.

30 There's a backlog of family members waiting for your care and attention. Get out your address book and call them up—it's long overdue.

OCTOBER

Monthly Overview

You need to deal with someone's emotional and sexual demands this month, and this may peak around the 9th. By sharing your dreams and desires around this time, you could give people a different perspective on who you are. Monetary issues between the 11th and the 23rd will cause you to be unavailable for your partner, but a small gift or gesture on the 14th can bridge the gap. The transit of Mars to your zone of domestic activities on the 26th indicates a push for independence or the creation of more space in your living area.

---

1 You start the month on an educational note as you are trying to expand your cultural understanding of the world. There may be connections with foreigners or other cultures today.

---

2 Debating the nature of the universe can be a lot of fun, but it can also waste a lot of time and make enemies. Try to keep your opinions to yourself.

3   If you're worried about hanging on to your job, it may be necessary to upgrade your skills. Although you are resistant to learning new techniques, you may be forced to do so shortly.

4   Usually you'd be overwhelmed by the amount of work you have to do, but today you have a great deal of energy and confidence to finish the tasks. You will feel a sense of accomplishment.

5   You could be beating your head against the wall trying to work out a technical problem that is better left to others. Don't let your ego get in the way of asking for help.

6   You have a great deal of creative imagination at present, so don't be afraid to step outside the square to showcase your unique qualities.

7   You're obstructed from functioning in the normal manner and you'd prefer to have a mini holiday today. Connecting with nature will recharge your batteries.

8   Even if you've received a bonus, you may find yourself playing catch up with bills. Try to curtail your spending habits and get back to a workable budget.

9 You're at your peak just now, and the Moon in Mars is offering you immense inner fortitude. Being a daredevil and doing something you ordinarily wouldn't is quite likely.

10 You want to make light of a situation. This is a good idea, especially if a relationship has become bogged down in too much seriousness. A joke will defuse the tension.

11 On the one hand you may feel sorrow over some sad news, but on the other you realise that the outcome is for the best. This is a day of mixed emotions.

12 If you notice waste in your organisation, the best you can do is be frugal yourself. A small contribution can make a big difference.

13 Your open and accepting attitude may attract a new person into your life. Although this is not a tactic on your part, it will work wonders.

14 This is day of assertion, and being strong will put you in a better position among your peers. However, breakthroughs can come at a cost, and others are feeling hard done by. You'll have to expect this.

15 You're probably confused about the internet and how you can use this to your advantage. This is a huge learning curve, but you have to start somewhere.

16 You should make some unusual preparations in your relationship, especially if you have been committed for a long time. If your relationship is unsettled, it may be time to make a big change.

17 You have intense mental strength today. Any task that requires clear perceptions will be favoured by the aspects of the Sun, Mercury and Mars.

18 Rather than feeling threatened by a junior in your workplace, try to work more closely with them. You also have talents they could learn from. A group effort works well today.

19 You can have a romantic or financial win just now. Perhaps a day at the races is on the cards.

20 If you're planning to travel, you need to get your documents in order. Get inoculations if you're planning to travel to Third World countries.

21 Flexibility will be a key ingredient in your negotiations today. This will show good judgment, and your speculative streak will continue today.

22 Holding on to a situation for the sake of a win is foolish. If this has been plaguing you, abandon or eliminate it now.

23 You're interested in novels, publishing and possibly even writing. It's an excellent time to put pen to paper.

24 It's an explosive day as the Moon, Mars and Venus bring your passion to a peak. Hopefully you have someone to share this with.

25 Dealing with a self-righteous person will cause pressure and anxiety today, but it's nothing you can't overcome. Try to come across as fair in your opinions. This way you can convert them rather than be converted.

26 Don't escalate a dispute today. Instead, narrow it down and stick to the point. This is the best way to remove the problem.

27 You are overinformed at the moment, and this is confusing you. Keep things as simple as possible today.

28 You have a big appetite now and may overdo things. You can still eat well, but remember to count the calories.

29 Your creativity is high, and this can be fed by your subtle perceptions, dreams and intuition. You need to set aside time to maximise these insights.

30 You're not in the mood to talk, but someone could force your hand. This will cause you to retaliate.

31 You may be offered a new position, but it's a horizontal leap that could lead to a more boring position. You need to balance more money with interesting work.

☽ NOVEMBER ☽

Monthly Overview

The month takes off positively with excellent communication on the 1st. Teaching, advertising and other forms of language fascinate you—and they will assist in achieving your goals. Your high level of energy around the 18th indicates conflict and arguments, and possibly even some mishap or injury. Don't overdo your exercise regime. Study, education and high-level discussions are likely around the 28th.

1 You could be overprotective, so don't react too strongly when someone muscles in on your turf. This is probably a sign of your insecurity.

2 You could make a new group of friends today and become emotionally attached to them. There may be humanitarian interests that are common to you all.

3 You're working well under pressure and you want to take on responsibilities that you would not have been able to handle earlier. This is helping you grow in confidence.

4 You need to draw the line when it comes to feeling compassion for others. They may be taking advantage of you.

5 Secrecy is your key word today, and you may not be able to divulge information that has come to hand. Others may not take too kindly to this, but it is professionally important.

6 You can make some breakthroughs in your work, but there could be competitive elements that make this a difficult process. Persistence will pay off.

7 You're able to share something of your past with someone who is like-minded, and you'll feel that they're unbiased and fair in their assessment of your problems.

8 Be careful of fuzzy wording, especially when it comes to contracts or business transactions. You're likely to be ill-equipped to sift truth from fiction.

9 You feel as if you can experiment and try something different now. For some of you, the stock market may provide an alternative way to increase you income.

10 You're eager to rock and roll right now, and fun times are on the cards. A night on the town with friends is likely.

11 You could feel numb from having to meet other people's standards. Be yourself.

12 What's required of you is changing, and you must find new ways of meeting other people's needs. Don't fall into the trap of being at everyone's beck and call.

13 Sometimes our families contain skeletons or hidden curses that burden us. You need to offload now and understand that you have the free will to change your destiny and family patterns.

14 You mustn't allow overconfidence to undermine your efforts today. Do things in a measured way for the best results.

15 Your positive thinking and high self-esteem can work wonders at present, but you may feel the pinch from family members who think you're growing faster than they are.

16 Although you may have a moment of clarity today, you need to know what to do with it. Planning your work and working your plan are operational musts.

17 Being decisive about your future may require a huge amount of courage and additional funds. Talk to your bank manager.

18 Your identity needs to change to conform to the demands of your workplace. This is necessary to survive the dog-eat-dog world we live in.

19 You want some peace of mind, but you may be badgered into going to a conference or study group. You'll have to make the best of this and extract what is useful for your own needs.

20 Curiosity killed the cat, and today your curiosity may lead you up the garden path. Try to read the signals before you invest too much time or energy into something that will be of no benefit to you.

21 Some of your friends are raving about the latest fads, but you can't see what all the fuss is about. Don't compromise your integrity for the sake of acceptance.

22 A cold reaction by your partner may be an elaborate tactic to steer you away from what's really going on. Delve deeper.

23 You've taken your eye off the ball, and your routine attitude to money is not going to cut it anymore. Try to establish where your income is going.

24 You need to make important telephone calls to solidify your position in the group. Cast aside the notion that your self-interest is selfishness. Rather, it can benefit others as well.

25 Inspiration is on the cards today, and it can be mutual. You may meet someone you look up to who feels the same way about you.

26 You may be focusing on the wrong thing today. Before you commence any work, make sure you gain clarity from those doling out the tasks.

27 If you're planning to do some work around the home or office, prepare yourself for some sort of assembled or makeshift shelter until the job is done. This will be of minor inconvenience for some time.

28 You shouldn't feel too bad if someone copies your manner or work. As the old saying goes, imitation is the greatest form of flattery.

29 You need to re-establish the bond between yourself and a close friend, particularly if that relationship has become frayed. Someone has to take the first step.

30 You could be a little obsessed by a relationship right now, but not for the right reasons. You need a time of separation to gain some perspective.

DECEMBER

Monthly Overview

Family affairs will take precedence this year, and Christmas will be a time when you reconnect with family members you have been disconnected from. Creating a more enjoyable home environment is likely. There may be an intense energy around the 15th when Uranus and Pluto challenge your domestic and family life, but clever communications on the 17th can smooth things over for a more harmonious Christmas.

1 You may disagree with an expert today, but you shouldn't let this bother you. Listen to their advice and trust your own intuition in these matters.

2 Sometimes you need to be a little subversive to gain the upper hand. If you notice that someone's behaviour is not in keeping with your standards, you may need to take action behind the scenes.

3 One of your key words now is discipline. It's not what you earn but what you say that's going to make the difference.

4 Someone in your peer group has information that is important for you. Perhaps you inadvertently missed a function or party where this information was revealed. You need to be brought up to speed.

5 Don't assume that your property is worth more than it is. You could be building castles in the air. Get a realistic market appraisal before planning your future security.

6 There could be a conflict of interest between your work and private affairs and you may not know which way to turn. The better aspects reveal that work should take priority.

7 Improved finances are assured right now. You can expect an increase in income, a bonus or an unexpected tax return.

8 You feel as if you have greater synchronisation today and may be able to read other people's thoughts—or so it seems. This is a day of sharing feelings.

9 You need to deal with a dominant person today, probably a female, and this could throw your whole day off balance. Maintain your composure and say as little as possible.

10 New partnerships can be arranged at present, but don't be disheartened if you experience some obstacles during the process. This may happen as a result of third parties meddling in your affairs.

11 You want things to move quickly today, so you may leave someone behind who's not pulling their weight. You can use today's planetary energies to get a head start on others.

12 If you make a mistake, admit your error and apologise for it. You'll appear bigger than you think in the eyes of others.

13 Misplaced affections may undermine your relationships, especially those of a romantic nature. All that glitters is not gold.

14 Someone may express their view in a way that embarrasses you in the company of others. You need to be less thin-skinned to handle these sorts of situations.

15 You feel as if anything's possible now that the Sun, the Moon and Jupiter are in favourable aspect. Neptune, the planet of vision and spirituality, is also channelling powerful energies for you to use. Dare to dream.

16 There's no harm in proving others wrong, but it's all in the way that you do it. Focus on form rather than content today.

17 Concerns over legal matters are short-lived, so analyse the issues carefully before making a decision. Compare opinions before setting your course.

18 Your passion for your lover is now underpinned by a sense of fun. Enjoy the energies of Mercury and Venus while they last.

19 An outing today could be fun but emotionally draining. Get lots of rest before embarking on your trip, especially if it involves some distance.

20 Your attraction is undeniable now. However, others may be expressing their feelings in order to get something rather than give it. Remember that.

21 Solitude will not necessarily give you peace of mind, particularly if you're brooding over some emotional matter. It's best to bring it out into the open.

22 This is a day of study and investigation, mostly of your own self. Psychology and philosophy may tie in with your past and explain why you've become who you are.

23 You are developing some new values, but fitting them into the structure of your day-to-day life won't be easy.

24 You may be tightening your belt while others in your family are spending freely. A new plan requires a joint effort from everyone, especially leading up to Christmas.

25 Merry Christmas, Libra! Mercury and Uranus indicate a wired, edgy sort of day, and the Moon in Mars adds heat to the combination. This is likely to be an intense Christmas. Get plenty of rest beforehand.

26 This festive season is full of social encounters, both new and old. By the end of day you are likely to feel emotionally drained. Don't do everything in one day.

27 Although you're in the midst of a crowd, you may feel disconnected from them. Perhaps the holiday season has shattered your nerves. Revitalise yourself through sport and a reconnection with nature.

28 Visits from faraway friends can be pleasurable at present. You may also connect with others by travelling to meet them.

29 The unexpected can happen with the Moon and Uranus in conjunction. Pleasant changes in your relationships are also forecast.

30 Your physical energy is strong, but your mental energy is diffused. This sort of planetary combination favours intense sports to relax your whole being.

31 The year finishes on a good note as the Moon makes excellent aspects to Neptune, the Sun and Pluto. You'll have an expanded awareness of the world and your community. You may also want to connect with others to help the less fortunate.

2014
ASTRONUMEROLOGY

TIME YOU ENJOY WASTING
IS NOT WASTED TIME.

Bertrand Russell

THE POWER BEHIND YOUR NAME

Everything in nature is ruled by numbers, including your name and birthday. By simply adding up the numbers of your name, the vibration and ruling planet of this number can be calculated, and through that we can study the effects on your life and destiny. There is an ancient system of numerology that originated in Chaldea. It is somewhat different from the system devised by Pythagoras, but it is equally, if not more, powerful and takes into account the planets and the effects on your name and birthday. Here is a table of the letters, numbers and ruling planets associated with them.

AIJQY	=	1	Sun
BKR	=	2	Moon
CGLS	=	3	Jupiter
DMT	=	4	Uranus
EHNX	=	5	Mercury
UVW	=	6	Venus
OZ	=	7	Neptune
FP	=	8	Saturn
—	=	9	Mars

Note: The number 9 is a spiritual number and, according to the ancient tradition of Chaldean numerology, is not assigned a letter. It is considered an unknowable number. Once the name or birthday numbers have been calculated, the number 9 is used as a sum total number for interpretation.

Throughout history, many people have changed their names for good luck, including actors, writers and musicians. They have done this in the hope of attracting good fortune by using the numbers of the planets connected with that birth date. If you look at the following table of numbers and their meanings, you will have a greater insight into how you can change your name and use this to your own advantage for more fulfilling relationships, wealth, general happiness and success.

Here is an example of how you can calculate the number and power of your name. If your name is Barack Obama, you can calculate the ruling numbers as follows:

B	A	R	A	C	K		O	B	A	M	A
2	1	2	1	3	2		7	2	1	4	1

Now add the numbers like this:

2 + 1 + 2 + 1 + 3 + 2 + 7 + 2 + 1 + 4 + 1   =   26

Then add   2 + 6   =   8

You can now see that the sum total of the numbers is 8, which is ruled by Saturn, and that the underlying vibrations of 2 and 6 are ruled by the Moon and Venus. You can now study the Name Number table to see what these planetary energies and numbers mean for Barack Obama. We can see from Saturn that he is an extremely hard-working and ambitious person with incredible concentration and the ability to sacrifice a lot for his chosen objectives. From Venus and the Moon, we see that he is a person possessing a delightful, charming and persuasive personality, and that he has a strong love for his family.

Name Number	Ruling Planet	Name Characteristics
1	Sun	Being ruled by the Sun means you possess abundant energy and attract others with your powerful aura. You are bright, magnetic and attractive as well. You are generous and loyal in disposition. Because of your high levels of energy, you need sport to make you feel good. You succeed in any enterprise you choose.
2	Moon	You are emotional and your temperament is soft and dreamy, but you must be careful of extreme mood swings. You are psychic and can use your intuitive hunches to understand others and gain an insight into your future. You have strong connections to your mother, family and women in general. Your caring and compassionate nature will make you popular with others.

Name Number	Ruling Planet	Name Characteristics
3	Jupiter	You seem to attract good luck without too much effort, but you must be on guard as you are likely to be excessive even when you are generous. You have strong philosophical instincts and wish to understand why you are here. Travelling is high on your agenda and you will explore many different facets of life and culture. You are a perennial student who wants to learn more about yourself and life in general.
4	Uranus	The number 4 is an unpredictable number, so you need to plan adequately for your life. It will have many unforeseen twists and turns, but you are extraordinarily innovative in the way you deal with life issues. You need unusual friends as you get bored easily, and it's quite likely you will take an interest in technological or scientific things. Learning to be flexible will go a long way in helping you secure a happy and fulfilling life.

Name Number	Ruling Planet	Name Characteristics
5	Mercury	Speed and accuracy are the key words for the planet Mercury and the number 5. You love communication and connect with people easily, but you need to be on guard against dissipating your energies into many frivolous activities. This is a youthful number, and you never grow old. You will always be surrounded by youngsters and people who make you laugh. You have a great sense of humour and will always be successful as you have the gift of the gab.
6	Venus	You have a natural inclination to love and be loved if you are ruled by the number 6 and Venus. Having a delightful personality, you attract many people of the opposite sex. You are successful with money and take great pleasure in working towards your future security. You will have many love affairs, and at some point you may even be torn between two lovers.

Name Number	Ruling Planet	Name Characteristics
7	Neptune	With the number 7 as your ruling number, you have reached a very high level of evolution. You are gifted with premonitions, intuition and clairvoyance. Health and healing are also gifts that you have been endowed with. Learn to discriminate when giving yourself to others.
8	Saturn	You have incredible focus and an ability to achieve anything you set your mind to, no matter how long it takes. You sacrifice for others as your loyalty is highly developed. You work hard to achieve things you believe are worthwhile, but sometimes this overshadows your personal life. You demand that things are done properly, which is why others may not be able to live up to your expectations. Learn to relax a little more.
9	Mars	You have a hot nature and need an outlet such as sport and other physical activities to balance your life and improve your health. You are not afraid of challenges and can be confrontational. Learn to listen and accept that others don't have the same attitudes as you. You are a protector of the family and loyal to the core. You are an individual and never follow another's lead.

YOUR PLANETARY RULER

Numerology is intimately linked to the planets, which is why astrology and your date of birth are also spiritually connected. Once again, here are the planets and their ruling numbers:

1   Sun

2   Moon

3   Jupiter

4   Uranus

5   Mercury

6   Venus

7   Neptune

8   Saturn

9   Mars

Finding your birth numbers is simple. All you have to do is add each of the numbers of your date of birth to arrive at a single digit number. If you're born on 12 November 1972, add the numbers of your day, month and year of birth to find your destiny number, like this:

$1 + 2 + 1 + 1 + 1 + 9 + 7 + 2 = 24$

Then add $2 + 4 = 6$

This means that the number 6, which is ruled by Venus, is your destiny number.

YOUR PLANETARY FORECAST

You can even take your ruling name number and add it to the year in question to throw more light on your coming personal affairs, like this:

B A R A C K O B A M A	=	8
Year coming	=	2014
Add 8 + 2 + 0 + 1 + 4	=	15
Add 1 + 5	=	6

This is the ruling year number using your name number as a basis. Therefore, you would study the influence of Venus (number 6) using the Trends for Your Planetary Ruler in 2014 table. Enjoy!

Trends for Your Planetary Number in 2014

Year Number	Ruling Planet	Results Throughout the Coming Year
1	Sun	

Overview

You are now ready to move forward in a new cycle and create something wonderful for yourself and your loved ones. Your career, finance and personal reputation will improve considerably and your physical health should also be much better. Although there may be some challenges, you're able to meet them head-on and come out a winner.

Love and Pleasure

You can attract anyone you want throughout 2014 because your energy and aura are so strong. You will need many friends and will find yourself doing creative activities alone and with others.

Work

You will have no problem getting a better job or some sort of promotion in your current line of work. More money can be expected, and any changes you make in your life should bring you great satisfaction.

Improving Your Luck

Good luck is on the cards, with July and August being especially lucky for you. The 1st, 8th, 15th and 22nd hours of Sundays are lucky.

Lucky numbers are 1, 10, 19 and 28.

Year Number	Ruling Planet	Results Throughout the Coming Year
2	Moon	

Overview

Although you will feel emotional this year, it's time to take control of yourself and change your personality for the better. Working through issues with females, both at home and in the workplace, may be the key to your happiness and success this year.

Love and Pleasure

Domestic affairs and relationships at home will take centre stage in 2014. Your marital relationship or important significant friendships are high on your agenda of things to improve. You are sensitive and intuitive, so trust your gut feeling when it comes to making decisions in this area of your life.

Work

Make your decisions based on rational thought rather than impulsive emotional reactions. Draw a clear line in the sand between work and leisure for best results. You are more creative this year, so hopefully you will take the opportunity to move along that path rather than doing something you are bored with.

Year Number	Ruling Planet	Results Throughout the Coming Year
2	Moon	**Improving Your Luck**

Mondays will be lucky and July will fulfil some of your dreams. The 1st, 8th, 15th and 22nd hours on Mondays are fortunate. Pay special attention to the New and Full Moons in 2014.

Lucky numbers are 2, 11, 20, 29 and 38.

Year Number	Ruling Planet	Results Throughout the Coming Year
3	Jupiter	

Overview

A number 3 year is usually a lucky one due to the beneficial influence of Jupiter. New opportunities, financial good fortune, travels and spiritual insights will be key factors in the coming year.

Love and Pleasure

You have a huge appetite for love, and bond easily with others to fulfil this need. Try to clarify your feelings before investing too much energy into someone who may not be the best choice. This is a year of entertainment and pleasure, and one in which generosity will bring good karma to you.

Work

You can finally ask for that pay rise as this is a lucky year when money will naturally come to you. Promotions, interviews for a new position and general good fortune can be expected.

Improving Your Luck

Don't let harebrained schemes distract you from the practical aspects of life. Good planning is necessary for success. March and December are lucky months. 2014 will bring you some unexpected surprises. The 1st, 8th, 15th and 24th hours of Thursdays are spiritually very lucky for you.

Lucky numbers are 3, 12, 21, and 30.

Year Number	Ruling Planet	Results Throughout the Coming Year
4	Uranus	

Overview

Expect the unexpected with this ruling number for the coming year. If you have spread yourself thinly, then you may lack the requisite energy to handle the changes that are coming. Independence is your key word, but impulse is also likely. Take your time before making important decisions, and structure your life appropriately.

Love and Pleasure

The grass may not be greener on the other side, and if you're feeling trapped in a relationship, you will want to break free of the entanglements that are strangling your self-development. You need to balance tradition with progress if you are to come out of this period a happy person.

Work

Innovation will help you make good progress in your professional life. Learn something new, especially in the technological arena. If you have been reluctant to improve your skill set, you are shooting yourself in the foot. Expand your horizons, learn new tasks and improve your professional future. Group activity will also help you carve a new niche for yourself.

Year Number	Ruling Planet	Results Throughout the Coming Year
4	Uranus	**Improving Your Luck**

Try not to overdo things this year and learn to be more forbearing with others. Slow and steady wins the race in 2014. Steady investments are lucky. The 1st, 8th, 15th and 20th hours of Saturdays will be very lucky for you.

Lucky numbers are 4, 13, 22 and 31.

Year Number	Ruling Planet	Results Throughout the Coming Year
5	Mercury	

Overview

You want to socialise and communicate your feelings this year because you have such a creative and powerful imagination, and it is likely you will connect with many new people. Try not to spread yourself too thinly, as concentration levels may be lacking. Don't be distracted by the wrong crowd.

Love and Pleasure

Reciprocation is important for your relationships in 2014. Variety is the spice of life, but also ensure that your key partnership will weather the storm and get stronger with time. Talk about your feelings, even if this is difficult. Don't be too harsh and critical of the one you love; instead, turn the spotlight of criticism on yourself to improve your character.

Work

People will look up to you in the coming 12 months, which is why new contracts will be drawn and doors will open to provide you with a bright new professional future. You are quick and capable, but try not to overdo things, as this can affect your nervous system. Travel is a great way to balance these energies.

Year Number	Ruling Planet	Results Throughout the Coming Year
5	Mercury	**Improving Your Luck**

Expressing ideas is essential and it will help you come up with great plans that others want to help you with. By being enthusiastic and creative, you will attract the support of those who count. The 1st, 8th, 15th and 20th hours of Wednesdays are your luckiest, so schedule your meetings and other important social engagements at these times.

Lucky numbers are 5, 14, 23 and 32.

Year Number	Ruling Planet	Results Throughout the Coming Year
6	Venus	

Overview

A year of love. Expect romantic and sensual interludes or a new love affair. Number 6 is also related to family life. Working with a loved one or family member is possible, and it will yield good results. Save money, cut costs and share your success.

Love and Pleasure

Love will be important to you, and if you are in a relationship, you can strengthen the bonds with your partner at this time. Making new friends is also on the cards, and these relationships will become equally significant, especially if you are not yet hitched. Engagement, marriage and other important celebrations take place. You will find yourself more socially active.

Work

You have a desire to work on your future financial security, so cutting back costs would be a key factor in this. You may find yourself with more money, but don't let false illusions cause you to spend more than you earn. Developing your part-time interest into a fully-fledged career is also something that can take place this year. Your social life and professional activities will overlap.

Year Number	Ruling Planet	Results Throughout the Coming Year
6	Venus	**Improving Your Luck** Developing a positive mental attitude will attract good luck and karma that is now ripe for the picking. Enjoy your success, but continue to work on removing those personality defects that are obstructing you from even bigger success. Balance spiritual and financial needs. The 1st, 8th, 15th and 20th hours on Fridays are extremely lucky for you this year, and new opportunities can arise when you least expect them. Lucky numbers are 6, 15, 24 and 33.

Year Number	Ruling Planet	Results Throughout the Coming Year
7	Neptune	

Overview

You have the power to intuitively understand what needs to be done in 2014. Trust your instincts and make greater efforts at your spiritual and philosophical wellbeing. This is the time when your purpose becomes crystal clear. You can gain a greater understanding of yourself and others and have the ability to heal those who need your help both within and outside your family.

Love and Pleasure

If you can overcome the tendency to find fault with yourself, you will start to truly love yourself and attract those who also love you. This is the key law of success in love, and you will discover this in the coming 12 months. Don't give more than others are prepared to reciprocate. You need to set your standards high enough to meet someone who is worthy of your love.

Work

This is the year to stop watching the clock and produce incredibly wonderful work. No matter how menial the task, you can experience the spiritual significance of work and how this can be used to uplift others. The healing, caring and social services professions may attract you just now.

Year Number	Ruling Planet	Results Throughout the Coming Year
7	Neptune	**Improving Your Luck**

Be clear in your communication so as to avoid misunderstandings with others. If you have some health issues, now is the time to clear them up and improve your general vitality. Sleep well, exercise and develop better eating habits to improve your life. The 1st, 8th, 15th and 20th hours of Wednesdays are your luckiest, so schedule your meetings and other important social engagements at these times.

Lucky numbers are 7, 16, 25 and 34.

Year Number	Ruling Planet	Results Throughout the Coming Year
8	Saturn	

Overview

This is a year of achievement, but it will require discipline and a removal of all distractions to achieve your goals. Eliminating unnecessary aspects of your life that constrict your success will be something you need to pay attention to. Your overall success may be slow, but it is assured.

Love and Pleasure

By overworking, you deny your loved ones the pleasure of your company and emotional support. Take the time to express how you feel. Remember that love is a verb. Spend more time with your loved ones as a countermeasure to excessive work routines.

Work

This is a money year, and the Chinese will tell you that the number 8 is very lucky indeed. But remember that money can't buy you love. Earn well, but also learn to balance your income potential with creative satisfaction.

Year Number	Ruling Planet	Results Throughout the Coming Year
8	Saturn	**Improving Your Luck**

If you are too cautious you may miss wonderful opportunities. Of course, you don't want to make mistakes, but sometimes these mistakes are the best lessons that life can dish out. Have courage and don't be afraid to try something new. The 1st, 8th, 15th and 20th hours of Saturdays are the best times for you in 2014.

Lucky numbers are 1, 8, 17, 26 and 35.

Year Number	Ruling Planet	Results Throughout the Coming Year
9	Mars	

Overview

This is the last cycle, which means that you will be tying up loose ends over the coming 12 months. Don't get caught up in trivial matters as this is the perfect time to redirect your energy into what you want in life. Don't be angry, avoid arguments and clearly focus on what you want now.

Love and Pleasure

You want someone who can return the love, energy and passion that you have for them. If this isn't happening, you may choose to end a relationship and find someone new. Even if you need to transition to a new life, try to do this with grace and diplomacy.

Work

You can be successful this year because of the sheer energy you are capable of investing into your projects. Finish off what is incomplete as there are big things around the corner, and you don't want to leave a mess behind. You can obtain respect and honour from your employers and co-workers.

Year Number	Ruling Planet	Results Throughout the Coming Year
9	Mars	**Improving Your Luck** Don't waste your valuable energy this year. Use it to discover the many talents that you possess. By doing this you can begin to improve your life in many different ways. Release tension to maintain health. The 1st, 8th, 15th and 20th hours of Tuesdays will be lucky for you throughout 2014. Lucky numbers are 9, 18, 27 and 36.

Mills & Boon® Online

Discover more romance at
www.millsandboon.co.uk

- **FREE** online reads
- **Books** up to one month before shops
- **Browse our books** before you buy

…and much more!

For exclusive competitions and instant updates:

Like us on **facebook.com/millsandboon**

Follow us on **twitter.com/millsandboon**

Join us on **community.millsandboon.co.uk**

Visit us Online Sign up for our FREE eNewsletter at **www.millsandboon.co.uk**

WEB/M&B/RTL5